Breakbeat Pedagogy

Studies in Criticality

Shirley R. Steinberg
General Editor

Vol. 512

The Counterpoints series is part of the Peter Lang Education list.
Every volume is peer reviewed and meets
the highest quality standards for content and production.

PETER LANG
New York • Bern • Frankfurt • Berlin
Brussels • Vienna • Oxford • Warsaw

Brian Mooney

Breakbeat Pedagogy

Hip Hop and Spoken Word Beyond the Classroom Walls

Foreword by Christopher Emdin

PETER LANG
New York • Bern • Frankfurt • Berlin
Brussels • Vienna • Oxford • Warsaw

Library of Congress Cataloging-in-Publication Data
Names: Mooney, Brian, author.
Title: Breakbeat pedagogy: hip-hop and spoken word
beyond the classroom walls / Brian Mooney.
Description: New York: Peter Lang, 2016.
Series: Counterpoints: studies in criticality; vol. 512 | ISSN 1058-1634
Includes bibliographical references.
Identifiers: LCCN 2016015059 | ISBN 978-1-4331-3325-1 (hardcover: alk. paper)
ISBN 978-1-4331-3324-4 (paperback: alk. paper) | ISBN 978-1-4539-1814-2 (ebook pdf)
ISBN 978-1-4331-3618-4 (epub) | ISBN978-1-4331-3619-1 (mobi)
Subjects: LCSH: Education, Urban—United States—Sociological aspects.
Hip-hop—United States—Influence. | Performance poetry—
Study and teaching—United States. | Culturally relevant pedagogy—United States.
African American youth—Education.
Classification: LCC LC5131 .M58 2016 | DDC 370.9173/2—dc23
LC record available at https://lccn.loc.gov/2016015059

Bibliographic information published by **Die Deutsche Nationalbibliothek**.
Die Deutsche Nationalbibliothek lists this publication in the "Deutsche
Nationalbibliografie"; detailed bibliographic data are available
on the Internet at http://dnb.d-nb.de/.

© 2016 Peter Lang Publishing, Inc., New York
29 Broadway, 18th floor, New York, NY 10006
www.peterlang.com

All rights reserved.
Reprint or reproduction, even partially, in all forms such as microfilm,
xerography, microfiche, microcard, and offset strictly prohibited.

*To my students
Past, Present, & Future*

*Well now you're forced to listen to the teacher and the lesson
Class is in session so you can stop guessin'
If this is a tape or a written down memo
In fact call it a lecture, a visual picture
Sort of a poetic and rhythm-like mixture*

–KRS-One

CONTENTS

	Foreword	ix
	Shout Outs	xiii
Chapter 1.	The Audacity of Breaking	1
Chapter 2.	A Nuyo Love	17
Chapter 3.	Breakin' It Down	27
Chapter 4.	*Word Up!*	39
Chapter 5.	Breakbeat Pedagogy	51
Chapter 6.	Writing as Breaking	61
Chapter 7.	Reading as Breaking	77
Chapter 8.	Speaking as Breaking	85
Chapter 9.	Pimping Butterflies and Teaching Stars	105
Chapter 10.	Future Breaks	115
	Appendixes	121
	References	145
	About the Author	149

FOREWORD

After decades of research that delicately pushed the boundaries of our shared understandings on the implications of race, culture and ethnicity on teaching and learning, the time has come for educators to face these issues head on and challenge the ways that schools, and those that work within them, have become complicit in the erasure of the culture of young people from teaching and learning. For decades, scholars have discussed race and culture without naming the ways that it has impacted curriculum, school culture, classroom structure, teacher recruitment, and most importantly, pedagogy.

Today, a new crop of scholars has taken on the charge to push unapologetically and challenge the ways that we shift both our understandings and our practice. Many of these scholars come from within the #HipHopEd community; a coalition of scholar-activists who emerge from the Hip Hop generation with a primary goal of bringing voice to marginalized groups they are in many ways still part of, while shifting theory and practice to reflect how race, class, culture and education intersect. This work has brought many #HipHopEd(ucators) to focus on the challenges of teachers who do not share the same ethnic, racial and cultural backgrounds as their students. We push back against the hyper-focus on theory at the expense of practical, tangible and sensible approaches to teaching and learning and do so without failing to engage with existent theory while reimagining who and what we pull from in order to develop new theories for how to improve education.

In this text, Brian Mooney imagines how theory and practice may merge in ways that privilege the unique cultural backgrounds of students. His theoretical and practical explorations of the breakbeat cover necessary new ground and exemplify what a new type of education work the #HipHopEd community is getting done. This work highlights aspects of urban youth culture that are overshadowed by commercial Hip Hop and undiscovered by disconnected educators who profess to engage in and with Hip Hop.

Those from within Hip Hop recognize the breakbeat as the heartbeat of the culture. It is the raw part of every Hip Hop song created by the deejay, the backdrop to which the b-girls moves, the soundtrack to late nights of graffiti writing, and the connection between Hip Hop culture and our ancestors who responded in their time much like we do to the boom and bap that are the raw ingredients of the breakbeat. What Brian Mooney explores in this text is the ways that the breakbeat is the backdrop to the event and how the event is the backdrop to good teaching. What he does is locate a phenomenon that is an anchor of Hip Hop (the breakbeat), and use it to highlight how youth construct identity, and how identity is then expressed in "the event."

The event is a significant teaching and learning space within Hip Hop that is at once used to inform the classroom in Mooney's work. The use of the event as an analogy of, or example for, the transgressive classroom space serves to position classrooms as we know them as emerging spaces that are far from complete or fixed in their form or function. This view of classroom as emerging pushes against ideas about the classroom having to look, feel, and sound in a single way. Breakbeat Pedagogy borrows from my work in reality pedagogy in that it considers the realities of the learner and functions to value experiential knowledge over given or taught knowledge. Its focus on literacy or Hip Hop Lit redefines literacy and what it means to be literate. It focuses on the sonic dimensions of literacy and positions poetry as the base from which all of literacy is birthed.

Some have described Brian Mooney and others' work that focuses on spoken word as existing outside of Hip Hop music/culture. They attempt to extract aspects of the culture that appear more polished or refined from the root it grows from. These attempts, which are couched in the ways that respectability and gender politics intersect with the performance of spoken word vs. Hip Hop/rap, are blocked by the nesting of the theories within this text in the breakbeat. As Mooney deconstructs media and socially constructed hierarchies between spoken word and Hip Hop, he challenges hierarchies between teacher and student, and troubles constructed hierarchies/tensions between white teachers and students of color.

Much of the gift that this text provides is showing readers how to own oneself and one's own privileges while doing revolutionary work. Brian addresses his Whiteness and Hip-Hop-ness and in so doing, models how "speaking onto the page" is an art he both practices and employs as a pedagogical strategy in the classroom. As he advocates for students to use their poetry to take their place as full citizens in a world that minimizes their brilliance, we learn that all who educate are required to envision a world where the classroom is simply preparation for the world beyond it. The students are to be equipped to transcend their immediate location and we are responsible for creating spaces where the breakbeat guides them towards emancipation.

Christopher Emdin
Teachers College, Columbia University

SHOUT OUTS

This book would not have been possible without God, my wife, family, friends, mentors, colleagues, and students. Shout out to my wife, Ani—I love you with all the light in my being. Special shout out to Michael Cirelli and Urban Word NYC for always believing in me. Huge shout out to Dr. Chris Emdin, whose brilliance, love, and mentorship have become a model for the kind of relationships I strive to maintain with the young people in my life. Thanks for reminding me to "stay low and keep firing." Shout out to the whole #HipHopEd movement, especially Ian Levy, Edmund Adjapong, Emily Bailin, Tim Jones, and Amil Cook. Shout out to the English Education Department at Teachers College. Shout out to my mentor at work, Mickey Diamond, the teacher I want to be when I grow up. Shout out to Allyson Krone, my vice principal, who has supported and encouraged me since day one. Shout out to the Performing Arts Department, especially Scott Killian and Rod Shepard. Shout out to all my students, to whom this whole book is dedicated. Shout out to Kendrick Lamar and Top Dawg Entertainment. Shout out to Jon Sands. Shout out to David Kirkland. Shout out to Yolanda Sealey-Ruiz. Shout out to Bronwen Low. Shout out to Kevin Coval and the Breakbeat Poets who gave me so much life and inspiration with their dope anthology of poetry. Shout out to Taylor Mali. Shout out to Paul Beresniewicz for the stunning cover art.

. 1 .
THE AUDACITY OF BREAKING

Hip hop is…the break beats you get broken with.
–Yasiin Bey (Mos Def)

Kendrick Lamar performs at Brian Mooney's school in New Jersey on June 8, 2015.

I Remember You Was Conflicted

When generational icon and Grammy Award–winning Hip Hop artist Kendrick Lamar visited our school, I kept thinking about all the schools around the world that deserved an experience like this, too. I thought about kids from neighboring Jersey City high schools who wished Kendrick were visiting their school that morning. I was simultaneously full of hope and despair. I felt a mix of gratitude and anger. As Kendrick says on his most recent album, "I remember feeling conflicted." That's because many schools, administrators, and districts are unwilling to embrace the educational potential of Hip Hop music and culture.

When Kendrick visited my classroom and listened to my students read poetry, he spoke about an experience in second grade when he used the word "audacity" correctly in a sentence. His teacher, astonished, told him he was going to be a poet. Jokingly, I asked Kendrick whether he had rhymed "audacity" with another word. He laughed and said no.

I find it ironic that "audacity" is the word Kendrick used in second grade. Audacity means "the willingness to take bold risks." In many ways, that's what teachers must do in the current climate of education. Teachers must take bold political risks in the classroom, pushing back against dominant ideologies that negatively affect our curriculums, schools, classrooms, and students. These are healthy risks—and they are absolutely necessary. People's lives and freedom depend on these risks. We must take them.

All teaching is political. Nearly every decision we make, from curriculum to method of instruction, is inherently embedded with political implications. The decision to include Kendrick Lamar in my curriculum called for an awareness of the racial turmoil that came to define 2015. It meant thinking about the #BlackLivesMatter movement and how Kendrick's release of *To Pimp a Butterfly* provided a soundtrack, a sonic landscape and backdrop, for what was happening in real-time on the streets of American cities and beyond.

The assumptions we bring with us into classrooms are political. Oftentimes, young people in urban schools are described as disengaged, unmotivated, and worst of all failing. But what if we are failing them? What if schools, in some ways, are set up for them to fail? Do we think it is purely coincidental that higher rates of poverty are directly correlated with lower graduation rates (American Psychological Association, 2012)? Are students of color less motivated, intelligent, or creative than their white counterparts?

As an educator who works with a diverse population of urban students, these questions, concerns, and contradictions continue to trouble me.

Although I have many questions, assumptions, and theories about the cause of the "achievement gap" (which is really an opportunity or access gap) and the challenges facing urban education, my work in public schools has confirmed one unavoidable truth: many young people are engaged in Hip Hop music and culture. Some might cite this as the cause of the problem I've described. However, I'm curious about the ways Hip Hop culture can be leveraged in classrooms and schools to engage urban youth in meaningful learning.

Later in this book, I outline the story of *Word Up!*—a Hip Hop and spoken word poetry event that I created with my students nearly five years ago. I then propose a framework that I call Breakbeat Pedagogy (BBP), which builds upon Hip-Hop–based education (HHBE) as a theoretical and practical framework for integrating Hip-Hop's elements into school communities more widely. This book combines different forms and styles of writing, including prose and poetry, in order to make a case for Breakbeat Pedagogy. This work takes the form of ethnographic teacher-research. Qualitative in nature, it relies primarily on narrative reflection and the analyses and interpretation of data. These data include student-writing samples such as poems, raps, and self-studies. Other forms of data include interviews, field notes, and video footage.

I wrote this book for a wide range of audiences, but particularly for teachers in urban schools who are curious about the practical applications of Hip Hop pedagogy. I've embraced my "classroom teacher voice" in order to highlight these practical applications. The pedagogies and theories I draw from are rooted in the context of my experience in the field. No knowledge or expertise of Hip Hop is required for reading this book. I do my best to explain key terms and lingo associated with the music and culture.

Back to the Roots

When I use the term "Hip-Hop," it will often be followed by the word "culture" because Hip Hop is a culture in the truest sense of the word. It has a rich and complex history with complicated social and cultural dimensions. Hip Hop is much more than just rap music. It was created by urban youth of color in the South Bronx during the 1970s (Chang, 2005) as a response to limited resources (Seidel, 2011), poverty, gang violence, and urban decay. Young people came together in community centers and schools in the hopes of ending gang violence and finding solutions to the borough's many problems. It was these young people, these innovators, who invented new ways of expressing their identities—initially through breakdancing, graffiti art, DJing, and rapping. These creative media became known as the original four elements of Hip Hop culture.

However, before the world came to know it as "Hip Hop," it was simply breakbeat culture. When DJ Kool Herc first realized he could sustain the energy of the crowd at local block parties and community gatherings by switching between two copies of the same record, isolating the instrumental portion of the song that was considered the "breakdown" or "break," everything changed. This new wave of sound and energy would ripple outwards for decades to come.

More than forty years later, Hip Hop has become a worldwide phenomenon, reaching every corner of the globe. In 2006, while visiting Berlin, Germany, I witnessed a thriving Hip Hop scene with open mic nights, concerts, and clubs filled with young people engaged in all four of the elements. What was once an exclusively urban American expression of culture and identity has become a global movement.

So how did a group of oppressed, marginalized youth from the South Bronx, living in poverty, with extraordinarily limited (external) resources, create a form of art so powerful and influential that it ultimately shaped a whole generation of people around the world? From where did their creative brilliance originate? Are the students in our classrooms today capable of the same creative brilliance and resourcefulness? What can teachers and students learn from Hip-Hop's birth story? These are questions I take up as I reflect on my own journey and work with young people.

Growing up in suburban New Jersey, just ten miles west of the Bronx, I was always fascinated with Hip Hop, even though I didn't look like, sound like, or identify with many of the experiences I heard in the music. My mother grew up in the Bronx during the 1960s and met my father there soon after he had emigrated from Ireland in the early 1980s. But like many white families taking flight from that neglected, poverty-stricken New York City borough, my mother's family settled in the suburbs of New Jersey in the 1970s. This was, perhaps, the first form of privilege that shaped my life.

As a child, most of my friends listened to rap music. It was on television and the radio. By the 1990s, I was a teenager and Hip Hop had crossed over into the realm of popular culture. It affected fashion, television, cinema, music, dance, theater—and transcended boundaries of race and class. Studies began showing that white Americans were the largest consumers of Hip Hop music and culture (Dunlevy, 2000).

It is essential that I discuss and reflect on my identity as a white male from the suburbs who works with Hip Hop in education. Many people claim Hip Hop is an art form created exclusively by and for black and brown people. This is true. In many ways, I am an outsider. Hip Hop is a cultural artifact that was created by Puerto Rican and African American young people from the South Bronx. It is a black art form and always will be. These are Hip Hop's roots and they shouldn't be dismissed simply because Hip Hop has become global and is now consumed by large numbers of whites. Hip Hop is a culture born of a specific oppression—as a response to that oppression—and there are some experiences inherent to Hip Hop that I will never understand. This becomes less problematic when I remember that students are the experts when it comes to Hip Hop.

Still, I must acknowledge the terms of my white privilege before I can do this work effectively. If white teachers are committed to working alongside oppressed people (Freire, 1970) in the fight for justice, we must consider all the social identity groups in which we have experienced privilege. For me, this means reflecting on my male, heterosexual, Christian, cis-gender, able-bodied privileges and how they've shaped my life (McIntosh, 1988).

White Privilege, Allies, and Hip Hop

Thinking about my role as a white "ally" (a term which I find somewhat problematic), or someone who works with and alongside oppressed people for social justice, is crucial to my research. I say work "alongside" because to imply a "rescuing" or "saving" of urban youth from a position of power and privilege is contradictory to this work.

The term "ally," while well intentioned, implies that the fight for justice belongs exclusively to someone else, *the other*, and that outsiders may simply align themselves with *the others'* cause through affiliation, but don't possess any real stake in the struggle for freedom. This perspective is shortsighted because it doesn't consider the notion that the oppressor is also harmed by all forms of oppression carried out in his name, against his brothers and sisters and countrymen and countrywomen. Oppression harms the oppressor and the oppressed. If white folks have benefited from our privileges at the expense of others (and we have), then consequently our freedom, dignity, and spiritual wholeness are compromised. I cannot be fully whole and free in a country that awards me privileges at the expense of others. This means that white teachers have a crucial stake in the work of social justice education. This means that both oppressor and oppressed have a stake in the collective struggle for justice. This is why I feel compelled to do the work of Hip Hop education from a place of authenticity, honesty, and humility.

It's true that, in the context of race, whites and people of color don't suffer in comparable ways. I am not claiming that my suffering is equal to the suffering of any other oppressed group. I am only suggesting that we think more deeply about the ways oppression harms all of us so that we might look for more openings for solidarity in our classrooms and beyond. I often think about James Baldwin's (1993) famous letter to his nephew in which he writes the following:

> [Whites] are in effect still trapped in a history which they do not understand and until they understand it, they cannot be released from it. They have had to believe for many years, and for innumerable reasons, that black men are inferior to white men.
> Many of them indeed know better, but as you will discover, people find it very difficult to act on what they know. To act is to be committed and to be committed is to be in danger. In this case the danger in the minds and hearts of most white Americans is the loss of their identity….
> [T]hose innocents who believed that your imprisonment made them safe are losing their grasp of reality. But these men are your brothers, your lost younger brothers, and if the word "integration" means anything, this is what it means, that we with love shall force our brothers to see themselves as they are, to cease fleeing from reality and begin to change it, for this is your home, my friend. (p. 8–10)

This passage has many implications for teachers. When I think about my responsibility as an educator, I'm reminded that reflective self-examination is hard work. It's uncomfortable. It's painful. It's like deconstructing walls that have been built and rebuilt for many hundreds of years, seeking to understand what (or who) is behind them, searching for our place in history, accepting that our place has obscured the place of others, and how many of those others are the students in our classrooms.

Baldwin's words don't offer a pardon, a pass, or a consolation. Rather, I feel called to "act" and "be committed," which as he reminds us, is to "be in danger." This danger prevents many well-intentioned white teachers from doing the inner-work required to "see [ourselves] as [we] are." We must refuse to "flee from reality." The primary task of twenty-first-century educators is working alongside one another for justice, freedom, and equity.

Hip Hop education, following in the traditions of Paulo Freire (1970), is built on a framework for educating oppressed people from the same place in which they live, work, and experience the world. If we find ourselves in a position of power and privilege, we then have a responsibility to help others empower themselves, working alongside them as we continue to strive for our own freedom and wholeness, always *becoming*, and never finished. This notion, more than anything else, has shaped my identity as a teacher.

Coming to understand and accept my own privilege is a lifelong process. My whiteness. My maleness. My heterosexuality. My cis-gender. My able-body. All of these identities have afforded me benefits and privileges that other groups of people have not been granted. If I want to work authentically with Hip Hop in education, I must come to terms with these privileges. I didn't ask for them, but I cannot return them. Therefore, in order to be part of the solution instead of perpetuating the problem through silence and complicity, I have dedicated myself to working alongside oppressed people from a place of honesty, humility, and authenticity. This requires continuous reflection and self-examination.

If I'm working with black and brown students, how can I effectively engage them in meaningful work using Hip Hop if I don't "keep it real" with myself—or in other words, keep it authentic? Young people are great at recognizing when people are disingenuous! It is essential that we are real with them. As uncomfortable as it might be, we must process the terms of our own privileges and reflect on what it means for us as teachers. This is perhaps the most "Hip Hop" thing we can do.

Social class is the only identity group in which I wasn't privileged growing up, although my current profession as a public school teacher has propelled me into the middle class, which now affords me certain social-class privileges. I grew up in suburban New Jersey, but my family was always on the fringes of the lower middle class. My dad was a construction worker who sometimes found himself unpredictably out of work—and after he and my mother split up during my sophomore year of high school, my mother had difficulty paying the bills on her secretary's salary. Our electricity was shut off on several occasions and for a time we had to get our groceries from a food pantry.

I don't cite these experiences to evoke sympathy or gain credibility as someone who "gets the struggle." But I use this example as a way to highlight the idea that we have all been the oppressed and oppressor in some capacity during our lives. It's important for us to think about the intersectionality of our identities. I understand financial hardship because of some difficult years without much money. I remember feeling a profound sense of injustice in 2008 when the banks wanted to foreclose on our home. I believe this allowed me to develop a sense of empathy for other people who are disadvantaged in similar and different ways. Thinking about power, privilege, and identity is fundamental to my role as teacher-researcher.

The beginnings of this study can be traced back to the 1970s when my family left the South Bronx. But I often think it can be traced back much farther, to when colonial Britain occupied Ireland, oppressing and dominating my ancestors with brutality. Even before I was born, colonialism was a force that began shaping me into the teacher I would become. I often wonder whether the history of my people somehow subconsciously heightened my sensitivity to the oppression of other groups, and has lent itself to my work in Hip Hop education. The Irish were eventually granted privileges in the United States (Ignatiev, 1995) that separated them from working-class people of color. These divisions have served to isolate us from one another for more than a century. Many of these racial and socioeconomic divisions have caused great rifts in our schools.

As I reflect on my identity, I begin to think about how I came to be here. My father was a construction worker who earned a modest income and there were some years we enjoyed the financial stability and privileges that accompany it. When my father emigrated from Ireland in the early 1980s, he didn't have a dollar to his name. No clothes. No family. Nothing. It would be easy for me to buy into the "bootstraps" narrative, claiming my father literally "constructed" our lives from nothing and that anyone, with enough hard work, elbow grease, and willpower, could do the same.

However, upon closer examination, it becomes apparent that even though my father was penniless when he arrived, he came with white privilege, welcomed to an America that had already predetermined his eligibility for certain privileges that were unavailable to other immigrants. He was accepted into the carpenters' union, which was, and is still, mainly dominated by Irish and Italian Americans. Would he have obtained a union membership and benefits if he had emigrated from South America? from Mexico? from China? from Nigeria? The answer is obvious. However, it doesn't detract from his years of hard work and sacrifice, for which I will always respect my father. I discuss this here to demonstrate that our identities are complicated matrixes and intersections, which began taking shape long before we arrived here. This identity work means opening ourselves to the dangers that Baldwin discussed. It means becoming vulnerable to our own histories. The result is an awakening of consciousness that must be initiated before we work with young people in the classroom.

Sleep / The Cousin of Death

The work of Maxine Greene, a scholar and educator whom I was fortunate enough to meet in the last few years of her life, continues to resonate with me. Greene's work and writings on aesthetic education—and her notion of "wide-awakeness"—speak directly to the work of Hip Hop education, which I take up at greater length in Chapter 3. The call for social justice embodied in Greene's work is often overlooked. She believed urban youth should be granted opportunities to have "aesthetic experiences" with the arts (Greene & Lincoln Center Institute, 2001, p. 106–107), just like their wealthy counterparts in schools with abundant resources and opportunities:

> [We must] expand our notions of what the domain of the arts includes. It means breaking down the old dichotomies, the separations between "high" and "low" art, between the arts and popular culture, even between the arts and those forms with their roots in folk or ethnic histories.... [This means] removing the arts from their pedestals and equipping all kinds of people to engage with them, to lend them their lives. And it means enlarging the domain of the arts so that all kinds of silenced voices could be heard, all kinds of once discarded imagery be attended to and, at the very least, explored.

Students in urban schools should have access to museums, performances, and other aesthetic experiences that enrich their lives through the arts. Hip Hop is a form of art that is already enriching many of their lives. There are infinite possibilities for culturally relevant teaching and learning if we are willing to reconsider the "discarded imagery" and discarded voices that have been relegated to the silent margins of our schools for too long. We must recognize Hip Hop and spoken word poetry as valuable artistic media that deserve a place in the classroom.

Labels like "street art" and "street poetry" often serve only to widen the chasm, elevating the pedestal of "high art" higher and higher, so that our students cannot possibly imagine themselves upon it. Our classrooms cannot continue to narrowly replicate the European wing of the museum if we expect our students to find their learning relevant and engaging in the twenty-first century. We must open the whole museum to them, even the wings we are not familiar with, even the ones students are constructing while we have been distracted in some cold dark gallery.

Wide-Awake (after Maxine Greene)
(a persona poem in the voice of the Metropolitan Museum of Art)

Dear New York City public school students,

I have never been able to tell you this, but I, too, am afraid of fire.
of decay. of time. of looting. of riots. of conquest.
It's how all my relatives died. It's how all my people perish.

You never learned this on any of those field trips to visit me
and you probably forget me right after descending my giant steps,
but at night, in the quiet stillness beside 5th avenue,
I have rummaged through your lost notebooks, backpacks, phones and iPods.
I have read pages and pages of your poems and raps,
thumbed through your black books
full of sketches and graffiti and love notes and confessions.
I am holding tight to a history they refuse to let me tell.

So next time you come back, do not donate anything.
Your admission has been paid in the currency of silence.

Sometimes, at the height of twilight,
I look north, beyond the park,
listen for the subtle hiss of aerosol
and watch you paint trains in the MTA yards.

Sometimes, I descend to the archives
and write rhymes with the rearranged lines of abstract expressionism,
16 bars for the kids who visit, just to leave an impression with 'em —
but you always leave without ever hearing my verses…
and some of them even got curses!

I just want you to know that my skin is a lot like yours.
I cannot control what people hang from it.

Last week someone left *The Autobiography of Malcolm* X in Gallery
548—European Sculpture, 1700–1900.
I watched security throw it in the garbage.
I wept that night, started this letter to you,
and haven't been able to sleep since.

Lately, everything inside me is too sterile, too glass case,
too clean, too passcode protected.
Lately, the marble galleries

seem to whisper in Aramaic
the words of a white Jesus adorned
in oil paint thorns
and temperature-controlled light
that costs more to install
than a park in your neighborhood.

"Father, forgive them, they know not what they do"
Forgive the adult untruths, false promises, tests, achievement gaps,
the sense of being human resources rather than singular persons and
participants in a community.

I just wish more of you would come back to visit me.

Memory.
An old woman told her students…"notice."
They did.
Curator told them no, no, see, context, intention, form,
and they stopped listening.

Old woman, flames in her eyes
burning with whatever it is that makes people alive.
Old woman only asking questions.
Old woman comes back so often I know every wrinkle in her skin….
Hasn't been back in a while though…

Before her, felt so misunderstood by the multitudes.
After her, seeking only to understand the multitudes better.
Every morning, been reading the 4,5,6 train as a text,
as a moving scripture,
as an urban ethnography of people whose stories I'm forbidden to tell.

Been thinking a lot lately about what it's like to die.
When I go, I want there to be ashes and falling rock,
broken marble, my skin bare as a newborn child's.
I don't want to go in my sleep.
I want to be wide-awake when it happens.

Knowledge of Self / The Metaphysical Cypher

Most classes start with a "Do Now" or "Warm-Up," but mine often start with a Hip Hop cypher. In a cypher, students stand in a circle, spread at equal distances, and one at a time each will contribute a rhyme, line of poetry, thought, idea, or affirmation. This circle is the pedagogical foundation of Hip Hop education.

On a recent February afternoon, just outside of New York City, only miles from Hip Hop's birthplace in the South Bronx, I asked my high school students to answer this question in the opening cypher: *Why should schools include Hip Hop in the curriculum?*

Eric, now a senior, insisted, "Hip Hop is a culture and it's just like learning about the Aztecs or the Mayans. We learn the origin, customs, and traditions of Hip Hop." Recalling a recent lesson on Hip Hop's "fifth element," Eric went on to explain, "Hip Hop offers students an opportunity to learn 'knowledge of self,' which is knowing who you are." It's important that Eric sees Hip Hop as a subject worthy of study with the potential to help students learn about themselves. Knowledge of self is a fundamental principle of Hip Hop culture *and* education. What does it mean to know who you are? where you come from? the history of your people? your family? the story of your name? These kinds of explorations are central to the work of teachers working in a postcolonial world. Our classrooms are amalgamations of cultures and identities, some of which have been violently obscured by dominant superpowers for hundreds of years. Before we can do the outer-work of looking at the world critically, we must do the inner-work of looking at ourselves. This is what we mean by knowledge of self. So what happens when we begin to look at the world through the lens of Hip Hop?

It's true that commercial Hip Hop is often sexist, misogynistic, homophobic, and violent. The same is true of contemporary cinema, television, sports, and American culture in general. This is precisely why we should create spaces for our students to critique these messages in the classroom. If we don't provide opportunities for students to think critically about the media they consume, who will?

Every year I teach a unit on sexism and masculinity in the media (Hurt, 2006), using Hip Hop as a lens to explore a variety of texts. I start by discussing with students a series of images depicting women in music videos, advertisements, and magazines. This year we considered an image of a famous rapper blatantly objectifying a woman in one of his music videos. This elicits quite a response from teenagers, as one can imagine, but almost always leads to an engaging, critical dialogue about the nature of sexism in Hip Hop and the media.

During this unit, students also consider the ways in which women are objectified on billboards and magazine covers, reading through a feminist lens while asking questions about the commercial motivations behind these images.

- *Who are these images intended for?*
- *Who makes decisions about advertisement content?*
- *What is the motivation of those who are trying to sell us these products?*
- *What is our responsibility as consumers of these images?*

We also analyze Hip Hop lyrics with the same questions in mind. We compare artists who glorify misogyny with those who offer us a counter-narrative, aiming to humanize women and critique the culture of sexism in Hip Hop and society. Artists we've studied include Lupe Fiasco, Kendrick Lamar, Mos Def, Queen Latifah, Lauryn Hill, and J. Cole (for a long list of educationally valuable Hip Hop songs, see Appendix C).

Hip Hop and Critical Media Literacy

When speaking with some educators, I'm often surprised that their perception of Hip Hop extends only as far as the radio. Many teachers don't realize the radio only broadcasts a corporate, commercial brand of rap music (Rose, 2008). There are countless other artists with positive, uplifting, and "socially conscious" messages, but they often go unheard. I think we should include both kinds of rap music in our classrooms if we want to have really meaningful, well-rounded discussions. We must be careful not to demonize rap music based solely on commercial Hip Hop. If we do, we are unintentionally enacting a form of symbolic violence (Bourdieu & Passeron, 1977) on students who identify with Hip Hop culture and consider it a part of who they are.

Oftentimes, in my classroom this kind of dialogue leads to powerful discussions about hyper-capitalism and the influence of corporations on the media we consume. One lesson in particular, inspired by educator and applied theater practitioner Anna Zivian, asks students to engage in a role-play in which they must assume the identities of corporate record executives presented with the task of signing one artist. Students must choose between a rapper whose lyrics are filled with violence, opulence, and degrading language towards women and a rapper who critiques these messages in a politically, morally, and socially responsible way. Ultimately students must decide in their persona as record executives, *What's more important—profits or people?* This is a political and moral question that should be taken up by all twenty-first-century citizens.

As an English Language Arts teacher, I'm tasked with helping students develop literacy skills. But what does it mean to be literate in the twenty-first century? What kinds of "texts" are relevant to students and how can we help them become more critical consumers of those texts? Breakbeat Pedagogy is a form of intervention that moves students from consumers to producers of Hip Hop's elements.

If we can agree that literacy means understanding and constructing meaning from the world around us, then popular culture, especially Hip Hop, represents a site rich with teaching and learning possibilities. Literacy in the twenty-first century extends far beyond the written word and page. The lives of young people are saturated with advertisements, music videos, films, video games, and blogs (Morrell, Dueñas, Gardica, & López, 2013). If we aren't helping students develop the tools necessary to think critically about these forms of media, we are doing them a disservice.

When we consider the influence of Hip Hop culture, for better or worse, on the young people in our classrooms, we are presented with an opportunity to engage urban youth in a way that speaks to their cultural identities while, at the same time, building critical literacy skills that are transferable to every other discipline.

As our classrooms become more and more diverse, we have a responsibility to address social inequities affecting urban youth. Sometimes this means the curriculum itself. Oftentimes, urban youth are described as disengaged and unmotivated, but what efforts are we making to affirm their social and cultural identities in schools? Hip Hop isn't the solution to every challenge in urban education, but it represents an important set of opportunities for meaningful, critical, and culturally relevant learning.

I've spoken a lot about identity in this chapter. One assignment that asks students to reflect on their own identities is the "Where I'm From" poem. I've written dozens of them with my students. I encourage you to write your own and to try this with students. So before we move on, let me tell you where I'm from.

Where I'm From
(for Ryan, after Willie Perdomo)

Because she liked the "kind of music" that I listened to and she liked the way I walked as well as the way I talked, she always wanted to know where I was from.

If I said I was from the Bronx, right in the heart of Woodlawn, where Guinness flowed like water and my pops had long hair in the 80s when he met my mom at the pub, do you think then she might know where I was from?

Or if I said that where I'm from was burning in the 70s and the landlords lit that shit themselves for the insurance money, you think she'd know where I was from?

Because I'm not really from there, see, I'm from white flight when the fires got too bright—when pop-pop packed up the car and the Europeans flocked across the Hudson like a second exodus.

I'm from a wake of destruction called the Cross-Bronx Expressway, slicing through communities like a hot knife through asphalt, buildings crumbling in my family's rearview mirror, when immigration part two meant—suburbs.

Where I'm from hip hop is a bridge—like the GW linked Bergen County and Washington Heights, but highway-hopped right over the hood, straight out to Long Island so white folks didn't have to feel uncomfortable when they vacationed in the Hamptons.

If I asked her, *you know how much moonlight it takes to break me?* you think she'd know where I was from?

Because I'm not really from there either, see, I'm from unpacking the six-step into a colonial two-step, shimmy shake the conquest right out of me, from Drogheda, whole town slaughtered by Cromwell, heads rolling down green hills like rotten potatoes.

Where I'm from, history stays on our minds like phone numbers before contact lists. I'm from Fordham Road shoe stores where Grandpa Kelly was a manager until the blacks pushed him out—is where they *told me* that I'm from.

But breakdancing and graffiti art is life where I'm from because the MC is just one element and where I'm from knowledge of self is a bible verse written in big fat bubble letters on parchment paper.

I'm from white kids who wanna be down but never flipped the record over to the dub side, never knew about sound system culture and resistance in Kingston, from history book bonfires, books with notes in the margins who are actually people you're not supposed to read about.

Or if I said I'm from Ireland would that be a lie? Even though every time I go back my cousins say, *"here comes the yank! welcome home lad!"* and embrace me with arms wide as an ocean—like the Atlantic really *was* just a pond between me and the motherland, like America wasn't an identity, just a place trying to find its own still.

I wonder, how could I show you where I'm from? White boy, hip-hop, can't stop won't stop, party block, college kid, occupy, ivy league, loan debt, teacher life, summers off, 9–5, more like 5–9, gas tank, almost empty, driving fast, Jersey Shore, windows down, salt in the air, grew up quick, rave scene, Brooklyn, warehouse, bass line, fill your chest, dance it out, overdose, dead friends, epidemic, on the news, no it's not, poor people, all unite, but they don't want us to, said they don't want us to.

So I told her I'm from here, by way of New York City, by way of Ireland, by way of Spain, by way of Africa. Told her I was from the West African talking drum, and she looked at me all crazy like, so I just told her—I'm from Jersey.

. 2 .
A NUYO LOVE

Breakbeats have been the missing link connecting the diasporic community to its drum woven past.
—Saul Williams

Student rappers perform at Word Up! in the Black Box Theater.

Spoken Word Democracies

I suppose the present story begins at New York University, where I took a course called Hip Hop & the Teaching of English. It was academically rigorous, thought provoking, and instantly blended my love of Hip Hop with my growing passion for young people and education. We read Paulo Freire, Gloria Ladson-Billings, Bakari Kitwana, Samy Alim, and many other scholars and cultural critics.

I soon discovered a discourse for teachers using Hip Hop and spoken word poetry in classrooms across the world. "Spoken word" is the art of performance poetry. Typically, this kind of art is performed at "poetry slams," competitions that ask members of the audience to help score poems and eventually crown a winner. The poetry slam has its roots in the 1980s in Chicago, where construction worker Marc Smith devised a clever way to get people into a bar to listen to poems (Aptowicz, 2007). Essentially, it was a ruse because the scores were irrelevant. It was the storytelling that mattered. Eventually, the poetry slam grew in popularity and came to New York venues such as the now-iconic Nuyorican Poets Cafe on the Lower East Side.

Several of my NYU classmates took me to the Nuyorican on a Friday night and I fell in love. I discovered that my quiet love for poetry no longer had to be so quiet. I heard brilliant, beautiful lines of verse being celebrated in a public space. People snapped their fingers, cheered, hooted, and hollered when they heard an especially powerful line. It was lively and engaging and somewhat unruly! I loved it. I didn't know it then, but the space I entered into that night would become a model for my future classroom. It was free. It was democratic. It was powered by the people in the room. There was no authoritative power directing things. It was a welcomed juxtaposition to the stuffy, elitist environment that characterizes much of academia. Soon I found myself in front of the microphone reading and performing poems on the Lower East Side, too. I began to see that, in many ways, spoken word *is* Hip Hop.

The First Year / When Are You Supposed to Smile?

After finishing my studies at NYU and continuing to think about the intersections of Hip Hop, spoken word, the poetry slam, and urban education, I got my first teaching job. It was here, at a public magnet school in Hudson County, New Jersey, that I would start trying to implement my ideas. There was some tension. There was some pushback. There were definitely some mistakes. But there was also lots of support, and eventually some great success.

I should take a moment to note that my school is a public school of choice, which means students from Hudson County are required to take an entrance exam. The school accepts approximately 10 percent of applicants. It is highly selective. We receive some of the highest-performing students in Hudson County, coming from Jersey City and Hoboken, to West New York and Kearny. Our school is extraordinarily diverse and was recently rated the third-most diverse school in New Jersey (Niche, 2015). The student population is predominately Latino/a, with white, black, Asian, and other ethnicities making up the remaining student body. Our students come from a wide range of socioeconomic backgrounds.

It's important to emphasize the "voluntary" and "selective" nature of our school. It's no secret that this population of high-performing students raises many implications for my research. How are these students different from the public school students in Jersey City or West New York (neighboring cities from which these students come)? What does it mean for them to "apply" and how does that influence their academic performance and potential? What kinds of resources, including supportive families, do these students have access to that others might not? These questions are full of assumptions and speculations, but they are necessary to consider.

I often describe my job as both harder and easier all at once. Harder because I have to continually find new ways to challenge these students, oftentimes thinking philosophically or reaching for college-level material, or risk boredom and disengagement—a challenge my colleagues in other urban schools know well. Yet my job is easier because there seems to be a sense of internal motivation on the part of these students and they typically have families who support them. They went through an application process, earned good grades in middle school, and showed a willingness to attend our high school. I'm careful about these assumptions, though, because I don't believe students in the local non-magnet high schools are less motivated, intellectual, or willing, or that they have unsupportive families. These differentiations can be harmful and divisive. I tend to think more about the similarities between my students and those at the local high schools rather than the differences. However, there are significant differences that surely affect the nature of this book.

The Slam Poetry Club

Fortunately, my administration has supported and encouraged me since the very beginning. I proposed two initiatives during my first year of teaching.

1. I started the extracurricular Slam Poetry Club (Tuesdays 3–5 p.m.).
2. I designed and taught an extracurricular course called Hip Hop Lit (Thursdays 3–5 p.m.).

This was more ambitious than I realized at the time, considering the demands of being a first-year teacher. Many colleagues joked about "surviving" the first year—and on many days it did in fact seem like a matter of survival! The never-ending lesson planning, writing curriculum, establishing boundaries, getting to know colleagues, talking on the phone with parents, and grading papers. It was overwhelming, but the extracurricular work seemed to rejuvenate me, keeping me grounded and inspired. It was my passion. Still, I wasn't sure how popular the club or class would be with students. After all, I was just getting to know them, too.

During the first week of school I discovered that over the course of the year the Performing Arts Department hosts several events called Coffeehouse Live during which students can sing or play music with their bands. It's a music event in our school's Black Box Theater, a small but intimate space that holds approximately two hundred people. One day in the teachers' lounge, the head of the Performing Arts Department heard that I had a background in performance poetry and asked whether I'd like to read a poem at Coffeehouse Live so the kids could get to know me. "How terrifying," I thought initially. But I've never been too afraid of the stage, so I agreed. Mr. Killian thought our school could use some exposure to spoken word poetry. At the time, there was no space for students (or teachers) to read or perform original writing for an audience.

Then it arrived. The second Friday in September of my first year of teaching. It was 3:15 p.m. and Coffeehouse Live was about to start. The kids didn't really know me. Neither did the teachers. But I was called up to the microphone in front of two hundred teenagers packed into the little Black Box Theater. I briefly explained to the wide-eyed audience that typically at poetry slams, if you hear a line you like, you can snap or respond verbally—as long as it's respectful and not too distracting to the performer! Then I read "Direct Orders (Shake the Dust)," a poem by my one of my favorite writers, Anis Mojgani, followed by one of my own poems. The kids snapped at different lines. They cheered. They went wild. Maybe it was just because a teacher had infiltrated their sacred Coffeehouse Live and was taking a big risk. Maybe it was because they really liked the poems. Maybe it was a combination of many variables, but the risk paid off. The kids loved the poems and it generated an initial spark of interest in spoken word poetry. It was only later I found out that teachers don't usually perform at Coffeehouse Live. Especially not poetry!

As the kids filtered out at 5:00 p.m. and headed for the late buses, a girl with green hair awkwardly approached me.

"Hey," she whispered timidly. "I loved the poem. I'm really into spoken word. We should start like a poetry slam club or something."

"Oh yeah? Do you think people would be into that?" I asked.

We made up some flyers and a week or two later held the first meeting of the Slam Poetry Club. I didn't have many ideas for activities or curriculum, but knew YouTube provides a huge archive of spoken word performances, so we started with that. With probably six or eight kids, we simply watched spoken word poetry on YouTube for the first few weeks. We looked at poets Taylor Mali, Sarah Kay, Saul Williams, Andrea Gibson, Buddy Wakefield, Lemon Andersen, and a host of others (see Appendix F for a longer list of spoken word poets). Oftentimes, I would read poems from my collection to the small group as we started to build a community around Hip Hop and spoken word.

Hip Hop Lit

Around that same time, during the fall of my first year, I started teaching my Hip Hop Lit course. While the Slam Poetry Club began growing on Tuesday afternoons, my Hip Hop class met on Thursdays after school. I wrote a curriculum for this extracurricular class—part of an after-school program in which students receive credits for taking elective courses approved by the district. My Hip Hop Lit class was approved and suddenly twenty students had enrolled. Now I had two groups of students, each with nearly twenty members who were interested in spoken word and Hip Hop. My initial description of Hip Hop Lit looked like this:

> The Hip Hop Lit course is designed to use hip hop as a platform for exploring social justice issues through a critical lens. Students will build high-level language arts skills while inquiring, critiquing, analyzing, and decoding lyrics, poems, social commentaries, news sources, and scholarly journals. "We will explore hip hop's conception and coming of age by studying its music and fictional works by hip hop generation

writers. One major focus is identity. We'll consider how claiming and creating identity remains an integral and urgent issue in hip-hop. We'll discuss the various elements of hip hop culture, but focus on rap and the poetic and narrative techniques it employs" (Gentry, 2012) in giving a voice to those who are otherwise silenced.

My primary inspiration for the Hip Hop course was Marc Lamont Hill's (2009) *Beats, Rhymes, and Classroom Life: Hip Hop Pedagogy and the Politics of Identity*, which is widely considered one of the first important texts in the emerging field of Hip Hop education. In his ethnographic study, Hill describes a course he piloted in an urban high school in Philadelphia treating Hip Hop texts as literature. The notion of Hip Hop as "literature" or "text" is itself political. What do we mean by "literature"? Does this refer only to the Great Books, the canon of European-dominated literature that most of us have come to know in our school careers? What happens when we think about popular culture artifacts like Hip Hop songs, music videos, and advertisements as "texts" that are worthy of study and analysis? What happens when we think about rappers as "authors" or "writers"? Freire and Macedo (1987) remind us that literacy means "reading the world" and in the twenty-first century it is more important than ever for students to gain the critical consciousness to think deeply about the media that saturate their worlds.

These questions and ideas, along with some other important texts in the field of Hip Hop pedagogy (Dimitriadis, 2001; Fisher, 2007; Low, 2011), helped frame my curriculum for the first year of Hip Hop Lit. In a slightly more formal setting than the Slam Poetry Club, this group would primarily study lyrics from artists like Dead Prez, Mos Def, Kendrick Lamar, J. Cole, Queen Latifah, Lupe Fiasco, Lauryn Hill, Tupac, Outkast, Common, and Nas, confronting topics such as sexism, misogyny, hyper-masculinity, cultural appropriation, and homophobia in Hip Hop. We typically started class with a cypher or some form of community building and then discussed social and political issues raised in the songs we studied. The course went according to plan (for the most part), but something unexpected happened.

The Open Mic Revolution

Before long, I noticed that in both the Slam Poetry Club (which met on Tuesdays after school) and my Hip Hop Lit class (which met on Thursdays after school), my students kept asking me for "open mic" time. This meant a period of five to ten minutes at the beginning of class reserved for anyone who wanted to get up and share something he or she had written, perhaps a verse, a poem, or a rap. They continued asking, week after week, so I listened—and scheduled time each week for "open mics." Now each club meeting and class started with an open mic, and they grew longer and longer. Both groups had about five to ten people read each week.

It soon became apparent that the room was filled with talented writers, producing brilliant poems on topics such as anxiety, divorce, racial identity, breakups, friendship, love, heartbreak, stress, and so much more. I wondered, *Was there no other space for students to tell these stories?* I began to integrate writing prompts into the curriculum so that students could respond creatively to the topics we explored in class. I modeled the kind of snapping and verbal affirmation that happens at poetry slams and it began to catch on. For months, all we did was listen, affirm, and support one another. I shared my own writing and poetry frequently. It's important for teachers to write and share their writing alongside students. Most of the poems students wrote didn't even require a prompt. They were simply writing about what was going on in their lives. They were writing their own stories. Eventually, we came up with a structure for generative writing workshops that centered on social justice–related topics, but in the beginning their writing was unprompted and done mostly out of school.

As my first year trudged along, an idea emerged right before the holiday recess. I'd made it to December (and smiled most of the way)! I found that my time after school with the Slam Poetry Club and Hip Hop Lit class was refreshing, and it provided less formal opportunities for me to simply *be* with my students. The after-school spaces were removed from some of the institutional daytime constraints like grades, deadlines, tests, administrators, and homework. We were there because we wanted to be. This is important because the extracurricular, voluntary nature of these spaces resembled what Dr. Maisha Fisher (2005) calls "participatory literacy communities," or PLCs.

These voluntary, community-based literacy spaces are similar to barbershops in African American neighborhoods, places where people congregate and engage in dialogue within a participatory context. The notion of PLCs also reminds me of Hip Hop's beginnings, when young people in the Bronx would stand in "cyphers" to rap or "spit" rhymes, taking turns contributing to the space. These participatory spaces juxtapose with the institutional nature of schools, the place were literacy practices are mandatory and regimented. Fisher talks about poetry slams as PLCs—something I've witnessed firsthand.

Oftentimes, before poetry slams in Jersey City and New York, I've watched poets writing together, sometimes over drinks or food, preparing for the slam. No instructor or teacher is leading them, but they are making a decision to write. There is a purpose to their writing: the slam. Teachers often require students to write but forget about the purpose for the writing. Will there be an intended audience? What is the occasion for the writing? Will the writing be received by peers, critics, or the public? What motivation is provided for students to really invest in the writing? The poetry slam gives them that reason.

Just before leaving for holiday break, one of my students suggested that "we should do an event in the Black Box Theater."

"You mean like Coffeehouse Live?" I asked (referring to the music event hosted by the Performing Arts students, some of whom had now joined the Slam Poetry Club).

"No, no," they said, "like a real poetry slam or Hip Hop event."

After some debate about what we should call this new event, *Word Up!* was born. We envisioned *Word Up!* as a celebration or showcase of spoken word poetry and Hip Hop culture, mainly featuring students rapping and performing poems. All that was needed was a microphone…and people to listen…and good poems…and a whole lot more we didn't yet realize. Nevertheless, the idea was a seed and it was planted in the winter of 2012. When we came back in January, we figured out how to make it bloom, regardless of the cold.

Yo Noobie
(after Jon Sands)

Yo first year of teaching—pshhhh.
Yo curriculum—of course Hip Hop is educational.
Yo Hip Hop—stop embarrassing me!
Yo standardized tests—how you expect me to fit all this creativity in that there bubble?
Yo rubric—how many points for empathy?
Yo lesson plans—why won't you cooperate?
Yo Race to the Top—your finish line looks different than mine.
Yo Kendrick—you make me want to like be myself forever.
Yo freshmen—stop staring at me like that.
Yo sophomores—you not THAT cool yet.
Yo dude in the supermarket who said teachers got it easy cuz we work till 3
and have summers off—check yourself.
Yo bags under my eyes—tell that dude in the supermarket that I'm in the
business of hopes and dreams and when you're on fire like this, sleep is hard
to come by.

A NUYO LOVE

Yo future self: you look like a dude who I could totally grow into, if only I knew the right combination of laughter and sin.
Yo midnight jungle of insecurities—this machete got a dull blade and I can't hack through all these faulty beliefs about myself.
Yo perfectionism—if you don't leave me alone I might just do something crazy like accept that I'm exactly where I'm supposed to be.
Yo integrity—I prefer waking up alone with you still intact.
Yo poets—if sharing your pain helps just one person, it was worth the suffering.
Yo love—I don't remember signing up for this.
Yo love—I'm allergic to everything except my daydreams of you.
Yo summer—I see you baby.
Yo swag—stop ruining everything.
Yo teenagers—this too shall pass.
Yo girl crying in the bathroom—he's not worth it.
Yo misogyny—"we all came from a woman, got our name from a woman and our game from a woman."
Yo Lasercat mascot—the chupacabra called and said you aren't real.
Yo front office—stop making announcements in my dreams.
Yo June—you the sexiest month on the whole damn calendar.
Yo yo! This is *Word Up!*

. 3 .
BREAKIN' IT DOWN

Break beat fanatic, crates deep in attics / Forty-fives marked up, looped with static
–GZA

The Slam Poetry Club.

The Hip Hop Art Space

I read the poem that concludes the previous chapter at our school's second-ever *Word Up!*—near the end of my first full year of teaching. I read last, after nearly twenty students had performed for a sold-out, standing-room-only crowd of excited teenagers, curious teachers, and semi-skeptical administrators. Getting to that moment was a process, a kind of coming-of-age story. It is the story of this event—the story of my students' development as writers—and the story of my identity as teacher-artist-researcher. These are the beginnings of Breakbeat Pedagogy, a kind of framework for teaching and learning that I hadn't yet named, centered on the Hip Hop performance art space.

When we returned to school in January 2013 to plan the first *Word Up!*, I decided to have a few joint meetings between the Slam Poetry Club and Hip Hop Lit class together as one group. Between both groups, there were over forty students who wanted to be part of the event. There are many ways for students to get involved in a poetry slam or Hip Hop event. We needed a DJ, someone to design flyers and artwork, ticket sales, promotion, social media managers, planning/organization, dancers, photography, music production, hosts, and many other roles that can be filled by students who aren't comfortable with performing.

When we recall the original four elements of Hip Hop culture (DJing, Rapping, Breakdancing, and Graffiti Art), a myriad of opportunities for participation emerge as possibilities for our students to get involved in a Hip Hop event. The elements of Hip Hop can be viewed as a multimodal framework for cultural production within schools. The elements represent multiple intelligences and capacities: Rapping (linguistic, verbal, oral, speech, auditory), Breakdancing (kinesthetic, bodily), Graffiti Art (visual, spatial), and DJing (technological, musical, audio).

Breakbeat Pedagogy is a cross-curricular philosophy of teaching and learning that moves beyond the traditional language arts approach to Hip Hop–based education. The Hip Hop event can be thematically adapted to meet a number of disciplines including science. Dr. Chris Emdin and the Science Genius Program (2016) demonstrate how students can learn S.T.E.M. content through the production of Hip Hop lyrics that deal with scientific concepts. This model could easily be adapted for other science-based subjects like engineering and mathematics, as well as the other humanities. Imagine a Hip Hop event that dealt with the theme of inequality. How might students produce artwork that deals with the statistics of mass incarceration and the private prison–industrial complex? What might that look like in the form of a rap, spoken word poem, choreographed dance routine, political graffiti art mural, or DJ set that samples different clips of audio? There would be countless opportunities to learn economics, history, science, mathematics, criminal justice, and law embedded in an event like this, for both the audience and the students participating. The Hip Hop event is multimodal and cross-curricular. The content can be adapted to the form and medium through which it is expressed. This preserves the essence of youth culture, equips students with new information and knowledge, and allows them to express their new understandings through cultural media that are familiar to them. This process begins in a classroom space that is open for students to talk about what is going on in their daily lived experiences.

In the weeks leading up to our first *Word Up!*, the open mics had grown so large that there wasn't enough time for everyone to share. Thus, *Word Up!* was the perfect opportunity to showcase the many powerful voices we heard after school each Tuesday and Thursday. I observed in my field notes when Rafi, one of the seniors during that first year, who describes himself as a rapper, singer, and songwriter, told the group, "Man, we need to show this school what's going on in here." *Word Up!* was our opportunity to create a performance space that transcended my classroom walls and invited the school community to come bear witness to the power of spoken word and Hip Hop. Putting this work on display is essential because we must champion the voices of young people. For us, this meant a performance event. Maxine Greene (2001) affirms the importance of "art spaces" that open doors of possibility and imagination to the community:

> We cannot but realize that teachers who have thought about their own experiencing, their own moments of joy, are the ones in a position to make significant choices where the arts are concerned. This is because they know in some profound sense; they have "been there"; they are committed to opening doors.... Teachers of this sort are likely to exert themselves in the creation of something resembling an art space in their schools; a space accessible to all kinds of children, to their fellow teachers, to the parents who come by. All depends upon a willingness to recognize how much engagement with the arts has to do with wide-awakeness, perceptual aliveness, the sense of discovery, the desire to learn and thereby go beyond. (p. 21)

Breakbeat Pedagogy means developing a Hip Hop art space in schools. Greene affirms the importance of teachers who are committed to constructing this space with students. These kinds of teachers will be people who are committed to doing the continuous inner-work of self-reflection and discovery in their own lives. Breakbeat Pedagogy asks us to open doors in a literal and figurative sense. When we create a Hip Hop performance art space, it's essential that the doors are open to the community, including family members, teachers, administration, and the local neighborhood. This kind of "opening" is contrary to the isolation and seclusion that often separate schools from the very communities in which they exist.

Because Hip Hop has existed for almost a full generation, many of my students' parents are old-school Hip Hop "heads." This is a new phenomenon that links two generations of people, much like the way rock 'n' roll of the 1960s began resonating with young people in the early 2000s. Today, millennials have parents who experienced the Hip Hop golden age of the 1990s. This is important because it creates a necessary pathway for student-parent engagement. This Hip Hop connection can be leveraged to involve parents and community members in the learning that happens in the twenty-first-century urban classroom.

The Hip Hop art space has the potential to engage urban communities in what Greene (2001, p. 21) calls "wide-awakeness." The performance event is conducive to this kind of awakening because it represents a metaphysical coming-together of bodies, ideas, artwork, voices, and experiences. When students gather in a theater or gymnasium to give voice to their experiences among the school community, a collective cypher is formed. There is an exchange taking place, as performers and audience members gain access to one another's experiences. Greene reminds us that these kinds of art spaces should be *accessible* to students and the community. Today, Hip Hop culture is probably the most accessible mode of expression available to students and their families.

Literacy as Performance

Blau (2003) talks about literacy as being "performative" in nature. He insists that "critical literacy" invites students to "aspire to full participation in civic and economic life for all citizens in a democratic republic" (p. 18). Blau's idea of performative literacy lends itself to Hip Hop culture, particularly the poetry slam event.

Literacy is a process of moments. It isn't a set of skills to be acquired or un-acquired. When students sit down to read or write a text, they are involved in a literacy event. Extending upon this idea and taking it to its logical conclusion, the poetry slam (or Hip Hop show) is the premier literacy event of the twenty-first century. Students invest in the writing and performance of their poems because of the event, and perhaps because of the audience and the anticipated reception of their work. There is a sense of "publishing" for the event. My account of the writing workshops that helped us prepare for *Word Up!* will reflect this notion further.

The poetry slam is an extension of an earlier literacy tradition—the Hip Hop event. In the 1970s, Bronx DJs Kool Herc and Afrika Bambaataa (Chang, 2005) hosted block parties where local youth danced, listened to music, and eventually rapped over the records. These Bronx community gatherings had a lot in common with sound system culture in Jamaica, but were essentially the first of their kind. The poetry slam can be traced back to ancient Greece or almost any culture with an oral history of storytelling. More recently, the beatnik poetry gatherings of the 1960s, which featured poets such as Allen Ginsberg, can be said to have heavily influenced the Hip Hop generation, as well as poets from the Black Arts Movement like Gil Scott-Heron, who laid down the bedrock of what we've come to know as spoken word and Hip Hop today. The poetry slam is simply the Hip Hop version of a very old tradition. The Hip Hop "battle," just like the slam, encourages participants to sharpen their skills and compete against one another in a healthy exchange of wit, bravado, and intellect. What many perceive as problematic confrontation is actually a form of therapy.

As I met with students to craft our version of the poetry slam, there were many decisions to be made. Should we use the slam format, with judges and scores and competition? How many students should perform? Should the event feature poetry and rapping? What is the role of music in the event? Should we focus solely on spoken word, without instrumentals and music? What kind of content is acceptable and appropriate? How much censorship, if any, is expected of us? How can we generate money to feature guest poets and teaching artists? We made all of these decisions together. I functioned as a facilitator, guide, planner, and mentor—but students were ultimately responsible for the event's success or failure. However, there was one thing I knew needed emphasizing. The event wouldn't be a success without good, strong writing.

Breaking Without Teachers

Leaning heavily on Peter Elbow's workshop model from *Writing Without Teachers* (1973), I demonstrated the kind of feedback we might use for writing workshops. I wanted these workshops to be organic, student-driven, constructive, confidence-building sessions wherein students could engage in "free-writing" to produce poems, and later, different forms of criticism such as "pointing, summarizing, telling, and showing" when providing verbal and written feedback to one another.

Pointing is the act of "pointing" to and saying back a line, word, or phrase in a text. It can be a line that speaks to you for whatever reason. Maybe it sounds good. Maybe it is especially beautiful or powerful. Maybe it's a simile or metaphor that jumps off the page at you. Pointing is a low-stakes reading and writing exercise that can help students notice what makes writing "good." I often tell students, "OK—when you listen to this poem, we're going to do a pointing exercise afterwards, so mark down words, lines, or phrases that stick out to you." Sometimes I tell them to look for "golden lines." This exercise is helpful in several ways:

1. It invites students to read closely.
2. It builds confidence in the writer who receives positive reinforcement.
3. It helps writers learn strategies from peers through exposure to their work.
4. It asks students to engage in "deep noticing."

Writing Without Teachers (1973) provides a model for writing workshops that are participant centered, peer driven, organic, and productive. Elbow outlines different kinds of feedback that can help a writer and those involved in the workshop. Here are some types of feedback strategies, which are outlined in detail in *Writing Without Teachers*, that I like to offer students in an Elbow-inspired workshop:

- Sharing (only reading, no feedback)
- Sayback (participants "say back" lines that speak to them)
- Pointing (described above)
- Summarizing
- What's Almost Said or Implied
- Center of Gravity
- Metaphorical Descriptions
  - Describe my piece in terms of weathers, clothing, colors, animals.
  - Describe the shape of my piece.
  - Give me a picture of the reader-writer relationship.
- Analytic Responding (traditional)

- Skeleton Feedback
- Believing and Doubting
- Descriptive Outline
- Movies of the Mind
- Criterion-Based or Judgment-Based Responding

Cookin' Up Breaks / In the (Writing) Lab

Elbow's workshop model is especially effective for generating healthy, productive feedback from teenagers who are helping one another write for a poetry slam or Hip Hop event. But before we can consider the feedback segment of the workshop, I found that as a writer, an identity that I value for myself, there was a lot to learn about the generative writing process.

How do we get kids to produce writing for a poetry slam in the first place? Lots of modeling is a good place to start. Watching YouTube videos of popular spoken word artists helps. And the importance of reading to kids can never be overstated. When developing a discourse community, students need to hear the sound of words and language. They need to absorb it. They need to consider the topics and themes that contemporary poets are writing about and then reflect on their own stories. *What story do you want to tell?* That is a question with infinite possibilities. It's a question that we should ask ourselves as teachers, researchers, and writers.

When I discovered Peter Elbow's work I didn't realize that I was already using many of his strategies with my students. Still, there was one idea that helped us all immensely—including my own writing. Free-writing is the act of letting yourself write without constraint. Oftentimes when we write, our brains are working in two conflicting capacities—producing and editing. Many of us can identify with the feeling of writing a line or two, thinking, "no, no that's not right," and deleting the line. This is an experience many students go through when trying to write a poem or essay.

Cognitive Load Theory (Sweller, 1994) suggests the brain has only so much capacity for intellectual activity. We can't produce and edit writing at the same time. When producing, we must free ourselves to wonder, rant, sidetrack, meander, go off on a tangent, return to an idea, wander, and imagine. This is a messy process! But I've found it's the only way for me to sit and write without the excruciating pain of second-guessing myself while staring at a blinking cursor on a blank white screen.

Free-writing is something than many teachers and students do regularly, but I believe it needs to be made explicit for students. The pedagogy and theory behind this kind of free-writing are important for students to understand. Conversations with students about the writing process recorded in my field notes revealed that many of them experience lots of self-doubt and won't let themselves produce the writing they are capable of producing. This is my story, too. I was once a struggling writer—mostly because I wouldn't allow myself to write. Once I discovered Elbow's approach to free-writing and what he calls "cooking," I was able to come back to my free-writing later, after the initial production process, and then do my editing, rearranging, and perhaps some further writing on ideas that needed some more "time in the oven." The Slam Poetry Club became a site for experimentation with free-writing and feedback. This freedom to experiment is crucial to Breakbeat Pedagogy.

Vernacular Breaking / Un-taming the Tongue

Elbow's latest work, *Vernacular Eloquence* (2011), is perhaps even more relevant for teachers who want to create a poetry slam or Hip Hop event. His central argument is simple: we can use the virtues of speech (the activity most people find easiest) to improve our writing (the activity most people find hardest).

He insists we must "un-tame the tongue" and "speak onto the page." Speaking onto the page doesn't necessarily mean using speech recognition software (although it can, and he talks about this technology at some length), but it's really a *mental gear*. We seem to have two gears for composing. The *writing mental gear* and the *speaking mental gear*. Elbow encourages us to use both, but argues for the speaking mental gear as a more natural, generative process, while the writing mental gear tends to stop us in our tracks, make us backspace, second-guess ourselves, edit, delete, and choose carefully what to say next. He wants us to enlist the natural, easy process of speaking with our minds directly onto the page, especially in the early stages of writing, in order to generate thinking without interference from the *writing gear*. Usually, we don't need the writing gear until later, during revision.

Speaking onto the page is inherent to spoken word and Hip Hop. Many poets and MCs compose this way, either off the top of their head, extemporaneously, or by drawing directly on the sound of language to compose in written form. After all, poetry is about sound. Students need to feel the words in their mouths. Spoken word is oral in nature. It's so similar to speech. This can be said of Hip Hop as well. Hip Hop and spoken word use language in ways that are pleasing to the ear (and to the mouth). If students can remove the roadblock of "trying to write a poem" and think about how to "speak the poem onto the page," we can unleash the power of the tongue and use speech as a tool for improving writing.

Workshopping the Workshop *(after Jon)*

With these ideas serving as the theoretical framework for the Hip Hop writing workshop, we began to actually "workshop" student poems. We created a schedule for the six weeks leading up to our first *Word Up!* event. Each week, about five student poets or MCs would bring in a poem or rap they had been working on, even if it wasn't yet fully developed. I usually suggest they have at least one page for the workshop. They must bring in enough copies for everyone in the group. (Usually the group is about twenty, unless it is a joint session with both groups, which might mean forty students, but that is typically too large for a good writing workshop. I think ten to fifteen students is the ideal range of participants in a writing workshop.)

In order to determine who would perform in the slam, we created a rule. The students who workshop their poem first would be confirmed and given a green light to perform in the show. If you were unprepared or didn't bring in copies of your poem for the group, you were red-lighted. This became a requirement and reinforced the importance of the writing itself. It would have been easy to haphazardly throw together an event of random student writing without giving much attention to the poems themselves. After all, there was a lot of logistical work that went into the event. But I was steadfast in my belief that the writing must be the focus. In my mind, without good writing (which is to say, clear, focused thinking), there is no event.

When a student comes in with a poem or rap (and copies for the group), here's how the session typically proceeds. These are the guidelines or "protocol" that I put on the board:

Workshop Protocol (General Guidelines)

- Respectful, Helpful, Considerate, Caring, Honest, Objective, Mature
- Feedback MUST be specific

- Remember, first drafts are supposed to be crappy!
- There is NO talking during the written feedback portion of the workshop

Workshop Protocol (Written Feedback Guidelines)

- Three specific **Warm** Comments (+)
- Three specific **Cool** Suggestions (−)
- Think about:
    - Figurative Language (metaphors, similes, personification)
    - Sound / Rhythm (alliteration, rhyme, meter, cadence)
    - Message / Purpose
    - Abstract vs. Concrete
    - Fresh Language

Breaking Down the Workshop

When a poet is ready to workshop, he or she starts by reading the poem in front of the group. The poet should NOT pass out hard copies of the poem until after the reading. I like participants to listen first, hearing the sound of the language, undistracted by the written text for the first read-through. Poets should read as if they were performing in front of the microphone (for performance tips see the next chapter). After reading, the poet passes out hard copies of the poem or rap. Then the group spends approximately seven to ten minutes providing written feedback. I emphasize that students must be as specific as possible. It's not helpful if a student writes, "I like this part." But it is helpful if a student writes, "This part is really powerful because you are providing a whole new perspective on sexism by switching between male and female voices." Of course, it would be wonderful if all our students could provide that quality of feedback all the time, but it usually doesn't start that way. It takes scaffolding. Sometimes it is OK for students to say, "I like this part." It builds confidence. It affirms the poet. It even shows a writer which parts most people enjoyed, and the writer can think about why. However, to really *grow* a writing community, good specific feedback should be encouraged. I would often model that kind of feedback in the beginning, until students learned how to do it on their own.

I require the written feedback portion of the workshop to be completely silent. This is one of the rare occasions when my classroom is completely devoid of sound! Usually during this segment of the workshop an observer could hear a pin drop. Students are highly engaged, reading and writing on each other's poems with ferocity. This is a consistent pattern that I've observed in my field notes. Students are invested in the storytelling process and they begin to see the value in expending energy on this part of the workshop. I almost never have to ask them to be quiet during this segment. The seven-to-ten-minute time frame is usually adequate for written feedback on a poem of one or two pages. I always encourage students to write at least three warm comments (+) and three cool suggestions (−). I use these terms because they are less aggressive than good/bad or strong/weak. Framing the feedback as warm comments and cool suggestions tends to keep the workshop constructive.

After the written feedback segment of the workshop, Elbow suggests allowing the writer to ask a specific question or two about her own work that she'd like the respondents to address. Afterward, the writer will not be permitted to speak. I've found that sometimes this works well and other times it doesn't. I like the idea of giving power, agency, and a sense of ownership to the writer before the group gives feedback. Sometimes the writer will ask questions like, "Did you guys get the ending?" Other times, "What did you guys think of this second stanza, does it fit?" Or perhaps, "Does this metaphor work?" This allows the writer to have specific concerns addressed right from the start. However, sometimes the writer will simply ask, "Well, what did you think?"

After asking their initial question, I find it important that writers are not allowed to speak. In the beginning, this meant I had to interrupt when writers who were receiving feedback wanted to respond to a participant. It becomes very tempting to defend your work when people are discussing it. You might want to justify your use of a certain word or phrase. You might want to explain a passage for clarity. But it's important for the writer to listen closely, taking notes if needed, and refraining from verbal response. This is hard for some students. But it has proven effective in allowing the group to generate healthy, peer-driven discussions without interference from the "creator." It's also an exercise in "close-listening" for the writer.

After the participants provide verbal feedback for approximately ten minutes, all of the hard copies, now with written feedback, are returned to the writer to take home for revision. This is the format we've used consistently and it has enabled us to produce some powerful writing. My role during the first year of doing these workshops was more of teacher, guide, and facilitator. Now, with some students who've been doing these workshops for four years, I can become more of a participant. Often, the seniors will facilitate the workshops, making sure things are moving along and even reminding writers, "No! You can't talk during this part!" or "OK everyone, be specific with your feedback!"

Teacher as Participant

I want to take a moment to discuss a deliberate decision that I made when participating in these workshops. During the second year, when I was able to become more of a participant, I sat in the circle and raised my hand when I wanted to offer verbal feedback to a writer. This might seem insignificant, but it reflects something important about Breakbeat Pedagogy. When preparing for a Hip Hop and spoken word event, teachers must depart from the banking model (Freire, 1970) of education in which, from the front of the room, teachers lecture, direct, speak at students, and essentially control the classroom. When a teacher sits with her students in a workshop and raises her hand to be called on by a writer asking for feedback, she has enacted an important power shift in classroom dynamics. This situates the teacher as participant / peer / member of the group. This has implications for my role as researcher, too. As part of the group, I have an inside perspective. It might be true that teachers will never be able to fully discard the institutional authority that is given to the adult leader of a classroom, but it's important to think about the ways we can move between roles and identities. If the writing group is going to become a community, there will surely be leaders, but it doesn't always have to be the teacher.

This notion of teacher as participant is fundamental to Hip Hop culture. In the cypher, there is no leader. It is a democratic space full of teacher-students. Sometimes I think the most Hip Hop thing we can do as educators is to relinquish control, humble ourselves, and let young people teach us for once.

. 4 .
WORD UP!

Two turntables, a mic, and breakbeat
–Erick Sermon

Poet Angel Nafis performs for a sold-out crowd at Word Up!

The Event: A Hip Hop Tradition

The name of our event, *Word Up!*, was the product of a group brainstorm. There are other events at our school, such as Dance Jam and Coffeehouse, Live so we wanted something "Hip Hop," something urban, something that could become our trademark event. There had never been a poetry or Hip Hop event at our school before this one. Some students participate in Poetry Out Loud, a statewide competition that asks students to recite classic poems and compete at the regional and state levels. Frankly, I've always found this competition boring. I think the recitation of poetry has an important place in schools and English classrooms, but it's a completely different event from a poetry slam that features students performing their own original writing. It's also true that Poetry Out Loud's selection of poems is lacking diversity. There are relatively few poets of color to choose from—and there isn't much "spoken word" or truly contemporary Hip Hop–influenced poetry available. This speaks to a larger trend by universities and other academic institutions that perceive spoken word and Hip Hop as "low art" or "street art." This hierarchy, as Maxine Greene (2001) suggests, is divisive and unproductive.

The other important decision we had to make was what format our event would take. Typically, poetry slams are competitions. There are usually several rounds in which judges, picked at random from the audience, will score poems, ultimately determining a winner. There are benefits and drawbacks to using the slam format in high schools. First, it's difficult to pick judges from the crowd if the audience is composed of teenagers. The judging of poems can quickly turn into a popularity contest and usually teens aren't yet mature enough to score poems as objectively as possible (even though full objectivity is impossible). The other option is to select teachers, parents, or administrators as the more "neutral" judges. This is also problematic because it shifts the power dynamics back to adults, introducing a level of judgment that comes from authority figures rather than peers.

If we think about the purpose of scores and judges in the context of the poetry slam's origins, it's clear these were measures meant to engage the audience and essentially "trick" people into listening to stories! However, it's true the scoring of poems can increase the level of competition among poets, as well as the engagement of the audience. Even though it's impossible to "grade" a poem, the notion still has value.

So why not use the poetry slam format? After all, won't the competitive element encourage kids to write better poems? This can be true, but I've found that the showcase or open mic format works better, and here's why. If a community of youth poets has become invested in the craft of storytelling, the enthusiasm is already contagious. There is no need for additional motivation, like scores, if student-poets, their friends, and the school community are showing up to support the event. If a "culture of listening" is established, and the shows are getting a good turnout, forget the slam format! The showcase format is ultimately safer and more open. While the slam format follows in the tradition of the Hip Hop battle, which enables participants to sharpen their skills in an exchange of verbal wit, the showcase allows for more possibilities of experimentation with event structure and format. It allows for more voices to be heard. Ultimately, the decision should be left up to students. I would suggest trying both showcase and slam formats and asking the kids which one they like better.

The other notable benefit of departing from the traditional slam format is the inclusion of music. Usually, poetry slams don't allow for any props or musical accompaniment, which closes off the event to rappers, MCs, DJs, and producers who make their own beats. I've found that including three or four "Hip Hop sets"—which could mean one or two songs each—in between poets works really well and breaks up the monotony of hearing one poem after another. Including the technologies of turntablism and beat-making ensures that one of the earliest and most fundamental elements of Hip Hop culture is represented in the event.

Departing from the slam format also means that Hip Hop dancers, breakers, or "b-boys" and "b-girls" can have a performance slot. Several of our shows have featured b-boys and b-girls who otherwise wouldn't have performed a poem or rap. This is important because it speaks to the multimodality of the Hip Hop event. Some students are kinesthetic learners and the event should include opportunities for them to perform an original choreographed breakdance routine. There might also be opportunities for students who produce graffiti art to perform in the show. I've seen poetry slams and Hip Hop concerts that feature graf writers composing live art pieces on the side of the stage over the course of the evening. This is a whole new visual and spatial element that opens up when we think beyond the traditional slam.

The structure of the event should vary depending on the needs of your students and the community. The following is a sample format that we've used for *Word Up!* This can and should be adapted. It can also be found in Appendix B.

Word Up!
Hip Hop & Spoken Word Event

1. Opening Poem
2. Introduction (MCs/Hosts)
3. Feature Preview
4. Poem
5. Poem
6. Poem
7. Poem
8. Hip Hop Set
9. Poem
10. Poem
11. Poem
12. Poem
13. Hip Hop Set
14. Poem
15. Poem
16. Poem
17. Poem
18. Dance Performance
19. Poem
20. Poem
21. Poem
22. FEATURE—(Guest Poet)—30 min.

It's important to open the space with a poem. We regard this opening as an opening of possibility, of unexpectedness, of invitation to the community. It is a symbolic act. It's tempting to address the crowd with long introductions and explanations of the program, but opening the space with a poem centers the event on youth voice. It's almost a ritual. What does it mean to "open a space"? It is a kind of breaking. When the poetry slam begins, we are breaking from the ordinary, the mundane, the monotonous, the standardized, and the predictable. Like a breakdancer, our movements are spontaneous, yet calculated. This is the essence of Breakbeat Pedagogy.

After the opening poem, we usually ask three or four student "MCs" or hosts to address the crowd. This is an opportunity for students to explain the structure and format of your event. This can also be a "mini-lesson" of sorts, allowing students to explain the origins of the poetry slam or Hip Hop event.

I usually ask students to talk about "the elements" and how they are represented in the event—through DJ / MC / Poet / Graffiti Artist.

The MC introduction is also a good time to explain that crowd engagement and interaction are encouraged! This could mean snapping, cheering, or responding with other verbal affirmations like "wowwww" when the crowd hears a line they like or that moves them. This is commonplace at poetry slams, but a student body might not be aware of these codes of conduct. This is another form of breaking from the white Eurocentric norms of school tradition. Typically in schools, students are expected to sit quietly without interrupting the speaker. This is unlike what happens in the black church. In what Dr. Chris Emdin calls "Pentecostal Pedagogy" (2016), the congregation is alert and attentive to the preacher. If the preacher feels the audience is becoming disengaged, he or she might ask for an "amen" or some other form of verbal affirmation. These traditions can be seen in the Hip Hop practice of call-and-response. When I say, "Hip" you say, "Hop!" These interactions are more than clever techniques to engage the audience. These are complex linguistic cues that are inherent to the African American oral tradition.

Schools primarily composed of white students might feel uncomfortable "interrupting" a speaker with cheers, snaps, or other verbal affirmations because of this cultural difference. However, in breaking with Eurocentric pedagogies, it's important to welcome sociolinguistic breaks into these kinds of spaces. Of course, it's also wise to remind teenagers that verbal affirmations should be respectful and positive, and ultimately strive for a balance that doesn't distract the performer from the task at hand— performing.

After the opening poem and MC introduction, we like to invite the featured poet, if we have one, to give us a little preview of what's to come later when he or she performs a full set. This preview is typically one poem. We've found this works well because it ignites the excitement of the audience, but doesn't overshadow all the student-performers who are about to perform.

As you can see from the sample format presented here, the opening poem and MC introductions are followed by student performances. I've found that a full show of two hours is usually enough time for twenty student performances of about two or three minutes each, plus a thirty-minute feature performance from the guest poet. It's usually a good idea to have the MCs introduce each poet very briefly, check in with the crowd, and have the DJ play some music in between poems. All told, this typically adds up to a full show.

There are many ways for students to get involved in the production of a Hip Hop or spoken word event: tickets, photography, video, artwork, social media promotion, sound, lights, stage management, music, and Djing. In this way, the "breakbeat event" is a multimodal production, drawing on the wide range of media and technological literacies that our students practice both in and out of school. The production of an event of this nature more accurately resembles the workforce environment of the twenty-first century. It requires collaboration, teamwork, technology, dialogue, problem solving, promotion, marketing, and a wide range of other skills that prepare students for experiences in the modern workforce. It's also important to note that the event doesn't need to conclude after the final poem. If students are recording their performances, they can be published on YouTube and shared widely. This provides an element of publishing that transcends the gym or theater. It's also a good idea to create an event hashtag on Twitter so that audience members may tweet their favorite lines or provide feedback about the show. It might also be a good idea to create a Facebook page or YouTube channel for your event. This provides a space for students to publish their poems even after the event is concluded.

The following is a list of roles and responsibilities that we assign to students in preparation for the event:

Roles & Responsibilities

- MCs/Hosts
- Promotion
- Social Media Managers
- Artwork
- Lights
- Sound
- DJ
- Flyers
- Tickets
- Tickets at the Door
- Video
- Photos

A Note on Guest Performers and Teaching Artists

If your school is near a metropolitan area, it's likely there are poets and MCs who will visit your school to perform and facilitate a workshop. The prices for these services vary, depending on such factors as time, distance, and popularity of the artist. Our Slam Poetry Club holds several fund-raisers such as bake sales to generate funds. Selling tickets to your event for $2 or $3 is also a good way to raise money to pay for a guest artist. It's important that you ask the guest poet or artist whether they can facilitate a workshop before or after the event. Typically, we hold these workshops before the show. Usually these are generative writing workshops to help students produce poems. Oftentimes, the poems they produce serve as material for the next show.

Standing Room Only

Since 2012, we've planned, produced, and hosted ten *Word Up!* events and one schoolwide event that featured Kendrick Lamar. The Kendrick event, which I discuss in Chapter 9, was in some ways the quintessential break. However, it was also just an extension of *Word Up!* in the Black Box Theater. Hip Hop and spoken word have the power to bring people together outside of individual classrooms. The energy of these shows cannot be captured in words. Consistently packing a theater full of people is no easy task. This is as much a testament to our student-poets as it is to the students who continuously show up to support and listen to them. I've always been astonished by this enthusiasm on the part of the audience. It says a lot about our school and kids.

Taylor Mali's Performance Tips

Before concluding this chapter with a poem that draws on multiple theories to crystallize my pedagogy in a kind of mini-literature review, I'd like to provide these performance tips courtesy of spoken word poet Taylor Mali, who many teachers might know for his piece "What Teachers Make." These are incredibly helpful tips for performers. I usually facilitate a workshop using these tips during the week or two prior to the slam. If performance isn't relevant for you and/or your students, skip ahead to the next section. I'd like to thank Taylor Mali for allowing me to publish these tips here.

13 Tips for Performing Poetry in Public

Adapted from Taylor Mali

1. Performance is an editing tool.

You learn things about your writing when you perform it. Don't think twice about going back and revising a section of your poem (or the entire poem!) based on the reactions (or lack of reactions) you get from a live audience.

2. Be an expert on the microphone.
Know how to adjust the mic stand in case you need to. Know where the mic should be and how close you should be to it. Remember that you have at least fifteen seconds to get ready before people will begin to wonder why you haven't started.

3. Clarity above all else.
If the messenger is not clear, then there really isn't any message, is there? You could be the most brilliant poet in the world, but if no one understands you they won't listen. Try over-enunciating, exaggerating the shape of your mouth with each word. You will not sound as stupid as you think you look.

4. Everyone wants you to be amazing!
Despite what you might think, the audience is not waiting for you to mess up. Nor are they hoping you do. They want you to blow them away with your words. So do them a favor and do so.

5. Have an interesting voice.
Or if you don't, at least use a fuller range of your voice than you would in a normal conversation. Get deeper in places and higher in others. Sing! I mean it! Include lines from songs in your poems and sing them, especially if you don't think you have a very good voice. The audience will love and admire you for having such guts.

6. Instruct or entertain or (if possible) do both!
Poets (like teachers) are part entertainers. Their poems should delight as well as inform. Put a little humor in most poems (even the sad ones).

7. Does a poem have to be true?
Not in the way an article in a newspaper or testimony in a court of law has to be true. You are allowed to change things here and there, use your poetic license, or even make things up if they serve your poem. Your poem should serve the larger Truth with a capital "T." It should be true to you even if it never happened.

8. Have a few lines that everyone will understand.
If you write "nonlinear" poems (more lyrical, imagistic poems that don't necessarily tell a story), be sure to have a few places where the audience can "rest" and think, "I understood that." If you don't, they will stop listening to you.

9. Never say, "I just wrote this poem today."

Because it means you either want the audience to be easy on you (because you're afraid your poem is bad) or be impressed by you (because you think it's good). Better to just shut up and recite the poem.

10. Go back to the nugget of truth.
Sometimes we get so caught up in trying to make our poems sound like poetry that we don't let ourselves say simple, truthful, beautiful things that would help the poem immensely. Things like, "Sometimes I wished I were an only child." Don't be afraid to leave the truth unadorned.

11. Stay still—or have a reason for moving.
Movement is usually the result of nervousness, and everyone can tell. Plant your feet and don't fidget. If you let your hands hang naturally at your sides you will LOOK normal (even if you FEEL stupid).

12. No one needs to know if you forget a line.
If your mind goes blank, take a pause. Don't let the audience know you have no idea what comes next. Start singing "Amazing Grace." Make up the rest of the poem as best as you can. No one cares that it's not perfect (except you).

13. Try to signal that the poem is over.
You know you have performed a poem well if the audience knows when it is time to start clapping simply because you start smiling. Don't be afraid to end with a moment of expectant silence. When they start to clap, stay for a moment and collect the applause before walking away.

An Anti-teaching Philosophy and Literature Review

Observation and participation / my favorite teachers / When they beat us in the head with them books / it don't reach us
–Dead Prez

Principals with no principles / Priorities political / Pedagogical planning is pitiful
–J-Live

The following poem is an "anti-teaching philosophy" and mini-literature review. As a persona poem, the speaker is "that" teacher who represents all (or most) of the pedagogies that I strive *not* to practice. It indirectly references some ideas that have shaped my beliefs about education by presenting the antithesis of those ideas in the voice of a teacher addressing his students. For an in-depth description and discussion of Breakbeat Pedagogy (BBP), skip ahead to the next chapter.

30 Days of American Schooling

1. This syllabus is now your God. Best learn how to genuflect. Everything is here in black and white. My expectations are clear. Don't act like you weren't told.

2. I will make my PowerPoints available to you every evening so you can study from them and absorb all this knowledge like a sponge. You will grow heavy and full with content that will be wrung out before ever fully absorbed.

3. Let's be clear. I am the teacher. You are the student. If you are ready, I will appear. If you are not ready, I will be marking your paper with red pen as the paragraphs bleed out into the margins. I will puncture the arteries and veins of your language until a pool of red ink drowns out your voice as you choke and gurgle on the grammar that you never learned because you already had your own.

4. Never say "I think" or "I believe" or "I feel like." No one cares what you think. Just eliminate those phrases and leave the ghost of what's left. Remain objective. Take yourself out of the paper as much as possible, but still remain. Write an argumentative essay without your opinion.

5. We don't speak like that in this school. Pull up your pants. Take off your hat or at least turn it forwards. Have some integrity. Speak proper English in this room. Speak a different variation of English. Yours is too versatile.

6. I don't know what goes on in this community after 3:00 PM because I drive to the freeway and go straight home.

7. We aren't going to talk about race, class, gender or privilege in this class. We are all the same. Equality, people. Ever heard of it? Just look – we have a Black president. This is post-racial America, so stop complaining.

8. When I raise my hand like this, that means quiet. I will count down from 3 – 2 – 1 and you will be quiet until you suffocate in the sweet symphony of silence.

9. We are going to learn respect if it's the last thing we do. You think you can act like that in the real world? If you talk like that on an interview, you'll never get a job. I'm trying to prepare you for the real world. You'll be thanking me in a few years.

10. Silence.

11. Silence.

12. Silence.

13. Let the silence rest on your tongue. Swallow it. Digest it. Let the absence of sound marinate in your gut until your throat burns with violence.

14. Oh don't even think about bringing that hip hop into my classroom. This is school. This is academic. This isn't the streets.

15. You call this a thesis? Get this out of my face and come back when it's provable and debatable. This isn't workable. A thesis is a way of life. It guides everything you do. Think of it like a savior, Thesis Christ.

16. Think of this school as a factory. I'm the CEO. The captain. The foreman. You are the worker. Scratch that. You are the product. We are going to produce greatness. You will be sorted and boxed and shipped to any university of your choosing, unless a legacy student gets in over you because their father donated a building.

17. Yes, why don't you "keep it real" and meet me in detention at 3:00. You can write on the board, "I will speak proper English" over and over again until you forget who you are.

18. Your experience means nothing here. Your personal connections to this text are irrelevant. See this? This is a literary criticism. You will write like this guy who majored in the study of Milton.

19. Participation is 50% of your grade but I'm going to talk for 75% of the time.

20. Does this make sense? Good. Great. Excellent. Moving on. We have a lot to cover.

21. This is not a democracy. If you don't like an assignment, too bad. Get used to doing things you don't like. It's called life. I have to show up here every day.

22. Check this spelling - there is no "u" in identity.

23. This draft is flat-lining. You killed it. It's dead. Perform an autopsy and bring it back to life. Stop daydreaming. Stop using your imagination.

24. I will not share my writing with you because I don't have time to write. Look how many papers I have to grade. You want to trade places? You can grade these papers while I attempt this writing assignment that I never placed myself inside of.

25. Think of reading and writing like divorced parents. You want to love both but they don't live together anymore and now you have to pick one.

26. Independent reading time is for kindergarten. This is high school. You will read at home, in isolation, because that's where learning happens. This is not story-time. I'm sorry, did you want a juice box?

27. Tie this poem to a chair and torture a confession out of it.

28. When we workshop someone's writing, make sure to pick it apart with a critical eye. Deconstruct it. Dissect it. Tear through it with your teeth like chicken from the bone. Slaughter it gently so the writer can pick up the pieces and re-assemble its corpse.

29. No questions at this time.

30. I have no answers.

. 5 .
BREAKBEAT PEDAGOGY

My break beat is to break away from yo thang.
—Arrested Development

Student DJ plays beats for the crowd.
(photo credit: Jose Flores)

Breakbeat Pedagogy: A Framework

The term "Hip Hop Hop–based education" (HHBE) has been used to describe the curricular and pedagogical uses of Hip Hop's four elements—DJing, Breakdancing, Rapping, and Graffiti Art. However, the theoretical and practical applications of HHBE remain unclear and there is sufficient need to question, clarify, and reimagine what HHBE might look like in schools. There is no shortage of critics who deem this kind of teaching and learning as "gimmicky," superficial, and ambiguous.

I propose a new framework, based on HHBE, which aims to clarify what this pedagogy looks like when a school more fully integrates the elements of Hip Hop via the performance art space. It is built on theory, but ultimately is based in reality. This framework is called Breakbeat Pedagogy (BBP).

Breakbeat Pedagogy is the art of the Hip Hop event. It involves the process of creating a poetry slam or Hip Hop event, alongside students, to initiate a democratic space for the elements to live and thrive within a school community. Hip Hop has a long tradition of "the event"—from South Bronx block parties to community centers to back-to-school jams at 1520 Sedgwick Ave. (Chang, 2005). "The event" is where the breakbeat first moved the crowd, united b-boys, and exemplified the performative, yet unpredictable and exciting nature of Hip Hop culture. Nowhere have the elements been more clearly on display than the Hip Hop event.

In order to clarify this pedagogy, I turn now to an important publication, *The BreakBeat Poets: New American Poets in the Age of Hip Hop* (Coval, Lansana, & Marshall, 2015), from which my book draws its name and its inspiration. It is the most comprehensive anthology of Hip Hop–generation poets ever published and an indispensable resource for educators. The following excerpt is from the section "Ars Poeticas & Essays":

> The *break* is the moment when everything in a song stops—except for the drums and bass or the drums alone. When Kool Herc, as we know, took two copies of the same record and spun the break back and forth, he extended the drum beat for as long as people on the floor wanted it to last. Thanks to Herc, the break wasn't just a fissure, a brief account, a short reprieve; it was the ongoing pulse, the call to what Afrika Bambaataa calls the Godself. Instead of thinking of it as a moment that comes and goes, the whole music was a sustained breaking. Herc changed the notion/the practice/the role of the break in history. He changed history, music as intervention, the ticks on the clock become the proverbial *break* o'dawn. (Rosal, 2015, p. 323)

Sustained Breaking

The break, manipulated by Kool Herc for the sake of dance, represents the most elemental nature of Hip Hop. When everything is stripped away, we are left with a drum pattern, reduced to its most simplistic form, yet infinitely complex in its implications for teaching and learning. The break, like storytelling itself, is fundamental to Hip Hop culture. If teachers and schools want to practice HHBE, I suggest looking back in time to what brought us all together to begin with—the breakbeat.

If the break is the moment when everything stops, we need to create pedagogical sites that suspend the space-time of traditional teaching and learning, looking to the Hip Hop event as the primary opportunity for us to honor the complex literacies, talents, interests, and stories of our students. The breakbeat is about unity, but also fracture. It is about harmony, but also discord. As Kevin Coval (2015) writes, it is to "break from the norm…a break in time…a rupture in narrative…a signifying of something new."

Events like *Word Up!*—the Hip Hop and spoken word event that I created with my students—represent the application of Breakbeat Pedagogy (BBP). The event, which features student-poets, MCs, graffiti writers, breakdancers, and DJs, is a communion of the elements both within and without. It exists inside the school, in the Black Box Theater, an institutional space, but it also exists somewhere between classrooms, between the officially sanctioned spaces, somewhere inside the breakbeat—a place uninterrupted by school bells and disruptive announcements.

The event is fundamental to BBP theory because it creates an "ongoing pulse." It isn't a momentary departure from traditional schooling, but a continuum of democratic unity, a metaphysical cypher that transcends the school calendar, giving students and teachers and parents a reason to come together. Like Kool Herc extending the break, the schoolwide Hip Hop event literally and figuratively extends the school day. It breaks or departs from previously charted waters, which scares many administrators and teachers. *What will students say with all that freedom?*

Word Up!—our Hip Hop event—symbolizes what Patrick Rosal (2015, p. 323) calls a "sustained breaking." It is a break not only from the institutional structures of the school day, but also from the scattered applications of critical pedagogues trying to implement HHBE in isolated spaces. It is a pedagogical coming together of the elements, generated by students, to celebrate, showcase, and champion youth voice. The Hip Hop event breaks from what Freire (1970) calls "the banking model of education" in a radical way. It positions the student as curator / presenter / teacher / storyteller / director / lecturer / organizer / and planner.

When students build a communal storytelling space—through poetry, rap, graffiti art, breakdancing, and even sonically, through DJing / turntablism—new kinds of incentives arise from the ashes of the archaic, rote methodology of Eurocentric pedagogies. Students begin to anticipate people showing up to listen. They know there will be a show, an event, a showcase, a reason to unite, a reason to stay after school and catch the late bus on a Friday because the slam team is performing and there's a guest poet coming from New York City that we've all seen on YouTube. They know someone will be working lights and sound, and selling tickets, and music will be playing—and there will be performances, entertainment, storytelling, a communal cypher that has been circulating since the last show, and which we are eager to continue.

Lights / Camera / Break!

The excitement surrounding a Hip Hop event is unparalleled. It is the essence of youth culture in a school. When student-poets and MCs know there is going to be a room or theater full of peers listening intently, there is a heightened level of motivation to perform well. The event is a catalyst for students to invest in the creation process. The real value is in the weeks and months leading up to the event, when students are engaged in critical conversations about race, class, gender, and identity. The real value can be found in the art-making process of workshopping poems, giving feedback, practicing performance techniques, refining stories, designing artwork, assembling playlists, and choreographing dance routines. This process is completely interest driven and student centered, with the teacher functioning as co-facilitator/planner.

Breakbeat Pedagogy depends on our willingness to embrace the idea that "flaws and fractures are the substance of imagination" and that "breaking is making" (Rosal, 2015, p. 325). When students and teachers create an art space that integrates elements of Hip Hop culture, there is a simultaneous breaking and building. Students, in their ontological vocation to become fully humanized (Freire, 1970), break from the structures and pedagogies that have been confining them to the margins of the classroom. Equipped with voice and microphone, their stories are a kind of shattering. They shatter preconceived notions about "articulateness" and literacy. They shatter stereotypes.

They shatter dominant narratives and ideologies that have excluded them. They shatter identities, rebuilding them in the same breath. Ultimately, they shatter despair and what Maxine Greene (1995) calls "the mundane." All these forms of breaking are also forms of building. But this kind of building can take place only in a democratic space that is open to the whole school.

Many schools and districts likely won't allow a "Hip Hop event." Sometimes we must frame the events as "poetry readings" or "poetry slams," which are essentially the same kinds of gatherings, but without the stigma of "Hip Hop." Until the powers that be will accept Hip Hop as a legitimate culture, we must find ways to transgress so that the work continues, regardless of those who try to silence us.

If there aren't facilities that can accommodate an event of this kind, a classroom, cafeteria, or gymnasium will do, as long as it can be opened to the community. Too often we relegate student performances to "presentation days" in our classrooms, limiting the performances to an audience of twenty-five or thirty peers. Our students are worthy of large audiences. This we know.

Bearing Witness

Breakbeat Pedagogy is a form of therapeutic intervention. It is a disruption of both form and content, interjecting itself into spaces previously closed off to Hip Hop, such as schoolwide assemblies in the gymnasium and shows in the performing arts theater. BBP sanctions a space for itself in a physical way. It reclaims the school building and says, "We're here in the spirit of peace, unity, love, and having fun." It says, "We're here on behalf of democracy." It says, "We're here to take over this theater and make it dope." It says, "We don't just study Hip Hop lyrics; we create and perform and showcase and invite the school to participate in our cypher, to build with us, and to come bear witness."

For participants in a Hip Hop community to bear witness there must be a physical coming together. We must exist in the same space with one another's bodies. BBP invites us to reclaim our bodies in a communal space. It channels the energy of a theater or gymnasium and translates that energy into snaps, moans of sympathy, verbal affirmations, head nods, and hands waving in the air. BBP reminds us that call-and-response works best when there's a crowd! BBP asks us to reflect on the moments that have moved us beyond our self-centered fear. BBP insists there is a power greater than ourselves at work when people come together in the spirit of unity. How we define that power is truly up to us.

I'll turn for a moment to the idea of the academic conference, a space in which professionals gather to share, present, build, and network. We know the feeling of the conference. It affirms that we are part of something. It's exciting to be in the presence of brilliant educators, people who share our vocation and our passion for teaching and learning. We sense there is an unspoken connectivity that materializes only when we come together in the physical. Many of us communicate via social media and participate in Twitter chats to share ideas and resources, but the ancient gathering of bodies in the same room prevails. Dialogue. Conversation. Listening. Performance. These things sustain us.

So what kinds of spaces do we create for our students to acquire this same kind of sustenance? It's true that some of our students attend out-of-school conferences such as Comic-Con, gatherings that bring together people who share similar interests, but why can't this happen in schools? Why must we make students leave their identities at the classroom door, forcing them to seek affirmation outside of the school building? Perhaps we should vacate our classrooms and head for the gym or theater. Perhaps our classrooms have served only to isolate teachers and students from one another, barring us from communal spaces that celebrate youth culture. This old design needs breaking. It needs reimagining. It needs poetry slams and Hip Hop events. It needs Breakbeat Pedagogy.

Critical Hip Hop Language Pedagogies

In my research, I have been particularly interested in the empowerment of school communities through Hip Hop pedagogy, spoken word performance, and the resistance to what Samy Alim (2007) calls "the language ideological combat that is being waged inside and outside of our classroom walls." We must recognize that waging a grammar war against speakers of different English dialects is an injustice, and that while most teachers devote exorbitant amounts of energy to cultivating an academic language, many students are busy "celebrating, highlighting, and consciously manipulating diverse language varieties" (Alim, 2007, p. 164). I have sought ways to celebrate this variety not only by integrating Hip Hop music and lyrics in the classroom, but also by employing the surrounding culture of graffiti art, DJing, breakdancing, and spoken word poetry in the larger school community. The synthesis of these elements is what I mean by Breakbeat Pedagogy.

Alim (2007) argues that "Critical Hip Hop Language Pedagogies, or CHHLPs, engage in the process of consciousness-raising, that is, the process of actively becoming aware of one's own position in the world and what to do about it" (p. 166). Breakbeat Pedagogy aims to develop this awareness, extending this consciousness-raising to the larger school community through the Hip Hop and spoken word event. Literacy is a participatory practice, a performative event in the truest sense, learned through critical and democratic social engagement in spaces that affirm identity, voice, and empowerment.

The use of Hip Hop in the classroom is not a simple gimmick disguised to get students interested in the literary canon (Morrell & Duncan-Andrade, 2002), although it can be used for that. The real value of Breakbeat Pedagogy is the dialogue it generates. Conversations about race, class, privilege, power, masculinity, and misogyny were common in my classroom when preparing for *Word Up!* This kind of dialogue speaks to the Freirean (1987) nature of Breakbeat Pedagogy because it asks students to "read the world" through a critical lens, developing a capacity for what Maxine Greene calls "wide-awakeness" (1995). The kinds of conflict that Hip Hop presents (Low, 2011) actually provide us with opportunities to confront oppression in a critical way, ultimately developing the capacities needed to become critical consumers and producers of texts in the twenty-first century (Low, 2011; Morrell, Dueñas, Garcia, & López, 2013). It isn't enough to have students engage in dialogue about sexism in Hip Hop. They need to produce a response, a reinterpretation, a talking back—and share these new understandings in a community space that extends beyond the classroom walls. We must invite the community, including administration, *into* our new understandings if our hope is for Hip Hop pedagogy to transform education.

Breaking the Common Core

One misconception is that Hip Hop and spoken word are not academically rigorous, when in fact the study of Hip Hop can be highly academic and aligned to the Common Core Standards. Morrell and Duncan-Andrade (2002) suggest that if we want to empower urban students to analyze complex literary texts, "hip hop can be used as a bridge linking the seemingly vast span between the streets and the world of academics" (p. 89). In my Hip Hop Lit class, we regularly engage in close-reading practices such as making inferences and predictions, identifying figurative language, analyzing theme, making connections, and synthesizing knowledge. One Common Core Standard that we address frequently is ELA Standard #6 under the Reading Literature cluster:

> CCSS.ELA-Literacy.RL.9-10.6 Analyze a particular point of view or cultural experience reflected in a work of literature from outside the United States, drawing on a wide reading of world literature.

Some would argue that Hip Hop texts, such as lyrics from American rappers, do not constitute "a work of literature from outside the United States." However, if we think about Hip Hop as a cultural artifact that has been shaped by colonialism and the African diaspora, we can understand Hip Hop as a cultural production that has always been "outside" the dominant narrative of the United States. The term "outside the United States" is open to interpretation. It asks us to consider the voices, identities, and stories of groups that have traditionally been silenced and marginalized within our borders, and within our curriculums.

It's also worth noting that Breakbeat Pedagogy meets many of the Speaking and Listening standards of the Common Core because poetry slam–style events carry on the oral tradition of Hip Hop culture. During a show, participants and audience members are engaged in an exchange that is dialogic in nature. There is a profound transaction happening between performers and audience members.

Dialogue as Pedagogy

Creating spaces to engage in critical dialogue with students has led me to believe that dialogue actually shapes the production of creative writing in a classroom and thus the event itself. Dr. Maisha Fisher (2005) observed a classroom in New York City that celebrated spoken word culture, calling the space a "Participatory Literacy Community" that allowed "students to be co-constructors of their learning community" (p. 116). My students and I constructed a similar environment through *Word Up!* I argue that this kind of shared literacy atmosphere is essential to our development as readers, writers, and performers.

The creative writing and performances that my students have demonstrated are coupled with empathy and awareness on the part of the audience.

Each week before the slam, my classroom is typically filled with snaps and cheers as students listen closely to their peers share original raps, freestyles, and poems. Most afternoons, the room is filled to capacity. We have created "a forum to expose and access multiple truths and experiences while fostering a particular kind of listening" (Fisher, 2005, p. 118). The listening itself is a literacy practice and the transactions taking place happen within that "culture of listening" (Fisher, 2005, p. 117).

Hip Hop fosters this kind of attentive listening and participation because young people are always waiting for the punch line. They want to be moved. They want to affirm themselves and one another. In my experience, the nature of student poems and raps is almost always positive, healing, and transformative when the space includes adults who are modeling this kind of writing and thinking. On the occasion when a student presented a poem that was sexist, homophobic, or violent, we were able to generate a dialogue around those issues to interrogate different perspectives, redirecting when needed, and using the experience as a learning moment.

Snapping represents affirmation, engagement, and participation in one another's literacy development. The result at our school was a growth of empathy that extended to the larger school community. At *Word Up!*, an observer would hear a cacophony of snaps and cheers in a theater filled to capacity with teachers, students, parents, and administrators.

My students spoke in what Patrick Camangian (2008) calls "a critical voice," which means "finding the power to be heard, felt and understood while communicating transformative ideas in ways that effectively impact and challenge listening audiences" (p. 39). Some students wrote poems about struggling with sexual identity, while others wrote about bullying and anxiety. It was common to hear sighs of identification, groans of sympathy, and cheers of celebration. As co-constructors of the event, students became the center of their own learning process.

If breaking is a form of "making," of "risk and mistake" (Rosal, 2015, p. 325), then the Hip Hop poetry slam is the ideal site for the practice of Breakbeat Pedagogy. When students approach the microphone with a story, they are both breaking and mending a part of themselves. Patrick Rosal (2015) reminds us that "an artist breaks only by being vulnerable to his own breaking" (p. 325). Breakbeat Pedagogy gives students an opportunity to "break into" experiences that have been previously closed off to them under lock and key. All we really need is one mic.

Mic Check
(a persona poem in the voice of a microphone)

When the spotlights are blaring
and their sweaty hands twist the stand,
lowering or raising me to their height,
I never get over how brave they are.
how infinite, how vulnerable,
to be made of blood and flesh,
how warm it must be to have organs
instead of metal in your chest.
I love the lights.
When they go dim that means
no one moving between whisper and scream,
no particles of spit being embedded
into my porous silicone membrane,
nothing to be amplified,
given volume,
translated into waves
and vibrations for ears.
I miss the way the freshman girl
always spoke her Ps too hard,
making me stab the audience
in the eardrum for a split second,
how I long to putter, pat, P, Puh, Puh,
grab me, hold me, lower me to your neck
and raise me again like a sunrise.
We are not so different—
both giving kids a way to tell stories,
adding volume to voice,
vividly inventing the very identity of everything.
I want sold-out crowds, listeners,
snaps, rhythm, volume, snaps, volume,
soft Ps, hard Ps, Ls, lots and lots of Ls,
whispers, shouts, screams, bass, thud, voice.
And when I die, I just want to go in front of someone's lips.

. 6 .
WRITING AS BREAKING

Broken glass everywhere
—Grandmaster Flash and the Furious Five

The slam team performs at Louder Than a Bomb youth poetry festival in Camden, New Jersey.

Allow Me to (Re)Introduce Myself

The next two chapters are presented as case studies of two students who have been members of the Slam Poetry Club and participants in *Word Up!* for several years. This chapter is a writer case study that focuses on a tenth grade student whom I've come to know through our work together. Eric (a pseudonym) was in the ninth grade when we first met. He was starting his first year of high school and I was beginning my first year of teaching. That fall, neither of us knew that we'd play an important role in the building of a writing community that would evolve into *Word Up!*

Explaining my relationship with Eric is not possible without describing the afternoon he surprised thirty students by speaking for the first time all year. In the weeks preceding the first *Word Up!*, we devoted entire afternoons to student workshops and event planning. The Slam Poetry Club joined the Hip Hop Lit class for several joint sessions, filling my room to capacity. It was especially full on the last Thursday before the event. I was finalizing the set list when Eric stood up in the corner of the room where some of the freshmen usually sat together. He held a stack of papers in his hand, approached me, and asked, "Can I workshop a poem and perform in *Word Up!*?" I was taken aback because I didn't know he wanted to participate in the event. I thought I'd included everyone, but somehow overlooked one last student who was ready and willing to share his writing. We had space for one more performer, so I asked the class to participate in one last writing workshop. What happened next was a defining moment for both of us.

Eric walked through a maze of students to reach the front of the room, clutching a poem in his shaking hands. Nearly everyone was surprised to see him standing there because he hadn't spoken all year. Not in discussions. Not in open mics. Not a word. But there he was, barely five feet tall, a freshman in a sea of strangers and upperclassmen, ready to speak for the first time in a classroom filled to capacity.

His height and age were deceiving because Eric read a spoken word poem that erupted from him like it had been waiting in his lungs all year. It was about being the quiet kid no one ever pays attention to. There were snaps and cheers. There were looks of bewilderment, mostly because it was so unexpected, but also because the writing was so powerful and his voice so confident. After an eruption of cheers and applause, Rafi, our senior Hip Hop star, jumped from his seat to hug and high-five Eric in front of everyone. This was our dramatic introduction to Eric:

Paper Trails
by Eric

Look at me.
A complex and quiet kid sitting at this table with people I am not even fond of.
My presence here is irrelevant and faint, it's like I'm not even here.
I try to get a sentence in but they constantly interfere.

I stop.

And stay quiet, trying again is another failure.
So I give up on these people and dive into the paper in front of me.
People surround me, but I can't help but still feel alone.
I am screaming inside, yet I don't make a noise.

Sadly, these blank pieces of paper are my only company.
Happily, these blank pieces of paper take me away from this reality.
Honestly, have you ever heard a word come out of my mouth before?
Or have you ever heard me speak like this?

I remember when I was young,
my mama and daddy were scared for me,
their youngest kid.
I didn't say a word or read a sentence,
my grandmother wanted to send me to a therapist.
I eventually said a word.
I even started to read.
I even made friends.
Though, there was still this empty feeling inside me.

Then I combined the paper and the pen.
Paper became my escape route from pressure, hate, and silence.
These papers on the table were my way to escape the violence.
In myself.
Struggles are constant inside and outside.
My outside problems may be easy to control and handle
But inside my troubles tear me apart
And I just can't help but feel like I'm the only one
in the dark trying to run toward relief
that isn't getting any closer.

What do I do? What am I saying? What is this? What is that?
It's basically just a bunch of what ifs and what ifs.

Oh man, here we go again, my thoughts run in circles
But then I force my pen upon the paper on the table.

I take refuge in the paper. Why?
Because that is the only place I am outspoken.
Those papers are the only place where I don't have to deal with interruptions,
just eruptions of my mind, thoughts, troubles, and struggles.
I write down how I try to follow morals and how I will sidestep the devil.

Paper is the place where I don't have to impress anyone
and there is no judge to judge.
Me.

The paper is the place where I don't have to put up this façade.

That is me.

These papers are who I am,
read them, and you will know me better than I do myself.
I am too confused to know who I am,
but once you read them you will understand
this lunatic inside this small body.

You can understand things just by reading a book, reading some lyrics,
capturing art, reading a poem, reading music.
Bottom line is, paper—it's there for you.

Eric speaks directly to his peers on that day in my room. His message is immediate and specific. It's a moment of "breaking" the previous silence that seemed to characterize his first year of high school. He is literally "breaking" out of silence and into voice. Writing becomes a form of nonviolence towards himself, a way to "escape" but also to confront the feelings of "pressure, hate, and silence" that afflict those who feel invisible and voiceless.

This feeling that "we're the only one" is common. The Hip Hop art space brings us together to exist momentarily within that feeling. Breakbeat Pedagogy means breaking from isolation and into collectivity, into unity, into community, into identification, and into healing. Paper becomes a refuge, a safe place, a place of voice and identity. But here, Eric himself is breaking that idea because we are watching as he is becoming outspoken off the paper, as well. He's putting sound to the voice on the paper and entering into a new space and a new stage of his development as a writer and performer.

If breaking is about risk taking, Eric is doing that here. He knows he won't be judged on paper, but he is opening himself to vulnerability, inviting us to move between the paper's lines, making the jump from silent, isolated writing to public performance. This poem is an honest self-reflection, not aiming to answer questions, but posing them. The paper becomes a metaphor for his experiences. And these experiences can be written, spoken, or both. Eric is doing both here. When he says "read them," he's really asking us to listen, closely and intently, with all of our hearts and spirits and being.

Paper is like a friend, a support, a medium in which to explore the self. It is a method through which he can name his experiences and reflect upon them. This poem, in many ways, represents the beginning of Eric's transformation from quiet, silent poet on paper to the confident, outspoken performer in the theater.

The Birth of the Poet

We laugh about that afternoon now that Eric has become a staple in the Slam Poetry Club. He's performed in nearly all of our *Word Up!* events. His family has come to see him perform and he's known as a poet in our school, an identity I asked him about and will discuss more subsequently. Some students even started calling him a "prodigy" and "the prince of poetry" because his performances are so powerful. At the second *Word Up!*, he received a standing ovation from a sold-out crowd in the Black Box Theater.

Even though I got to know Eric and his writing during that first year, I didn't have him in English class. My only interactions with him occurred in an extracurricular context, usually after school. I wondered how this affected our relationship, if at all. Fortunately, my relationship with Eric was able to grow and I had him in class the following year. Sometimes I saw him during the day, for English class, and then again after school at the Slam Poetry Club. Although this may have shifted the power dynamics of our relationship, it has also allowed me to know him in a variety of different contexts. This has provided me with the opportunity to explore his writing in greater depth.

Eric became part of a group of students who wrote in a Daily Writing Discipline notebook, posted commentaries about literature on the class blog, and reflected on their writing in audit reports at the end of each marking period. I learned all of these methods in a graduate course called The Teaching of Writing. We were also fortunate enough to be invited to Teachers College in January 2013 for the second annual Hip Hop Youth Summit, sponsored by the Institute for Urban and Minority Education. Since my research on writing has been shifting to focus on the construction of identity, I required each student attending the summit to submit a "writer self-study." All of these data, including Eric's Daily Writing notebook, audit reports, writer self-study, and the poems he wrote for *Word Up!*, have allowed me to make reflective, interpretive insights into the way a young writer's sense of self is shaped by and evolves within a supportive Hip Hop writing community.

Can I Kick It?

Although I had a wealth of writing to analyze, I wanted to meet with Eric for a short interview to learn more about him and to reflect on our experiences together with Hip Hop and spoken word. On Monday, February 10, 2014, I met with Eric for an interview that I recorded on my iPhone. We reviewed the scope of my research together and I was completely transparent with the process. I explained the use of pseudonyms and asked whether he'd like to choose one. We met in my classroom, at my desk, during a free period. I closed the door, which is usually left open, but some students roaming the halls interrupted us a few times. However, our discussion went smoothly and I had some questions already prepared.

Meeting in the classroom has both positive and negative effects. Because this space is where we've done nearly all of our work together, it provides a sense of comfort and familiarity. But in this space, particularly at my desk, it seems impossible to transcend the institutional power that has been granted to me in my role as teacher. Eric makes this clear when he admits, "This year, since I actually have you as a teacher I kind of see you more like an authority." This troubled me at first, but this dynamic has its benefits, too. This project is an academic one. It is based on research, analysis, and interpretation. My role as researcher doesn't necessarily conflict with my role as mentor. In some ways, it enhances and strengthens it. This kind of work might change the way Eric sees me, moving from mentor-poet to academic-researcher, but these roles are fluid and interchangeable. Just as students are capable of style shifting, so too are teachers and researchers. I would hope that my decision to involve Eric in this research gives credibility to our work with Hip Hop and spoken word, and that he sees the connection between the Black Box Theater and the academy. Perhaps I have to detach from the writing community of which I've become part in order to conduct more objective research, but I think Eric understands and respects this dynamic. If anything, it adds legitimacy to our work together.

In our interview, I learned about Eric's academic background and his experiences in middle school. He told me, "I was silent. I never talked. Like you could probably go throughout the day, and you would probably forget I was there." This strikes me because it parallels his first few months in Hip Hop Lit and starkly contrasts with the evolution of his "performance-self." I wonder how many other students feel invisible and never have an opportunity to remind a community of listeners that yes, they are there. I'm always bewildered when I see a quiet student on stage in the theater, performing in front of a crowd. They seem temporarily to adopt a new identity. On that afternoon when Eric surprised us with his poem, it was impossible to forget his presence. His writing was immediate and alive. It had a voice. It was undeniably present.

You Can Get with This / Or You Can Get with That

When I asked Eric about his hobbies and interests, he cited writing as his primary hobby. I wondered whether this was a new development or something he'd always considered a hobby, so I asked about his connection to Hip Hop in the past. Eric informed me that he started listening to Hip Hop in the sixth grade as an attempt to "fit in with the guys." Now he listens to different "styles" of Hip Hop, suggesting that he differentiates between subgenres and styles such as "socially conscious Hip Hop and commercial Hip Hop." Eric defines himself as "a poet that is a part-time author and part-time MC" and declares, "I cannot consider myself anything higher than a writer."

Eric is playing with the definition of "writer" here. In a creative writing assignment for English called "The Random Autobiography," he writes:

> I used to want to be a crossing guard,
> an actor, a singer, an artist, a poet,
> a rapper, an author, a rapper again,
> and now I want to be a poet,
> but I still attempt to rap, sometimes.

This playful movement between labels suggests that Eric sees good writers as versatile in their movement between identities. His biggest fear is "writing the same thing over and over again." During a workshop in the Slam Poetry Club, I observed in my field notes when a student pointed out that Eric "always writes in the same style." Many of his poems deal with sexism, beauty, and self-worth. In one of his audit reports, he cites this experience as a motivator, claiming, "My Daily Writing notebook changed because of that. After hearing that comment, I wanted to try to experiment with different styles." Eric took the comment seriously enough to alter his writing on a daily basis. The Daily Writing Discipline is space where he can "experiment with different styles." All students of writing should have a space to do this. Eric shows that he is reflective and willing enough to apply suggestions, especially from his peers.

The Risk of Breaking

Our goal for this study grew out of our interview discussion. I proposed a starting point: *How can we continue to grow together in our work with Hip Hop and spoken word poetry?* I wanted the question to be vague so that we had room to think about something more specific. In our conversation, Eric kept returning to his biggest fear—"writing the same thing over and over again." He clearly expressed a desire to experiment with different styles, voices, and trajectories:

> [W]riting the same thing over and over again is like one of my biggest fears…. I don't want to be known as like the sensitive guy, like how Drake is the sensitive rapper…. I don't want to be the one known for writing about women and like how they feel…. I want to be known for writing.

Eric is thinking about how others see him as a writer, but also how he sees and understands himself. This level of metacognition suggests that Eric may have internalized the identity of "writer" and understands this identity isn't fixed or absolute. His desire to change the way he's perceived suggests a level of agency. He wishes to represent himself in a way that is acceptable, gratifying, and authentic *to himself*. What's meaningful here is that Eric *motivates himself* to grow beyond his current state of being. Yet, this passage also reveals a conflict. Even though Eric's poems about "women's issues" have received standing ovations at *Word Up!*, he battles with the hyper-masculine expectations that are often reinforced in Hip Hop culture. Even though we regularly challenge socially constructed identities in our writing and discussions, we can see here that Eric is still resisting certain identities, particularly when he tries to explore what "kind" of writer he wants to be.

Co-constructing Group Identity

Toward the end of our interview, I asked Eric again, "*Moving forward, how can we grow together in our work with Hip Hop and spoken word?*" He responded with a particularly profound question. Eric asked, "Grow as a writer, or as a community?" The fact that Eric sees growth as happening on both the individual and group levels brings up more questions about identity. *How can a community of writers negotiate the collective identity of the group? How does individual identity shape the group identity? How does the group identity impact the individual identity?* I started to think more about the collective identity of our writing community and its implications for Breakbeat Pedagogy.

Eric and I agreed that part of our long-term goal should not only address individual writing ambitions but also speak to the group's development. We decided that our goal should be to expose each other to and experiment with as many different voices, styles, perspectives, and forms as possible. We agreed that many "slam poets" start to sound the same and ultimately become confined by the expectations of the genre. This happens in Hip Hop, too. Therefore, we planned to read and write a more diverse array of poetry to avoid the monotonous expectations and limitations of genre.

Rocking the Mic Right

I want to analyze Eric's participation in *Word Up!* This is the experience that evoked the most positive response from him during our interview. He called his first performance a "defining moment" for him as a writer—and in many ways it defined my first year as an educator. Breakbeat Pedagogy—the process of starting a writing community, workshopping poems, planning an event, and opening the doors to the larger school community for the exposure to Hip Hop's elements—has changed my beliefs about writing in particular. The success of the event and the process leading up to it leads me to believe that participatory writing communities, like the Slam Poetry Club, are essential to the development of young writers. I often think about the ways I can integrate the positive elements of the extracurricular writing community into my daytime courses.

In a writing assignment for Hip Hop Lit, I asked students to hypothetically defend the course to the board of education, arguing for its continued inclusion in the district curriculum. Eric, who was enrolled in my Hip Hop Lit class that year, wrote extensively about *Word Up!*:

> One of the most impacting events was definitely *Word Up!* It not only allowed us to show our talents but [also] our views on social issues, ourselves, and our goals…. We used what we learned in class and put it into the way we speak and the way we perceive things. The class allows you to hear the opinions and views of others…. You're able to think in a way where you aren't naive. That's why I believe our event was so successful. We really knew what we talking about, we really believed in what we were saying. When we say something…I think that's the way we challenge the conceptions of hip hop being [only] homophobic and violent.

Much of the curriculum in Hip Hop Lit was aimed at what researchers call Critical Media Literacy (Morrell, Dueñas, Garcia, & López, 2013). Our discussions centered on topics such as racism, sexism, heterosexism, and hyper-masculinity in Hip Hop and society at large. Usually, these lessons included a creative writing component at the end of class. I wondered how the curriculum shaped the nature of the creative writing that students produced. Would the analysis of lyrics and discussions about hyper-masculinity influence the creative writing of students? Would dialogue influence their thinking and "reading of the world" after class was over? How can a researcher measure this? I sensed a definitive connection between the nature of our lessons and the writing generated by students. However, I wasn't sure how to prove this. I theorized that the learning process looked something like this:

1. Lesson on a relevant topic / problem (i.e., homophobia in Hip Hop and society)
2. Close-reading and analysis of a mentor text (i.e., lyrics, poem, or article)
3. Guided discussion / open dialogue
4. Creative writing to synthesize, interpret, and/or challenge ideas
5. Sharing / open mic
6. Workshopping a poem
7. Performance at event

Although this might seem prescriptive, there is much to be said about the effectiveness of this structure. I think the key here is that students benefit from the freedom to write and express their own ideas on a topic that is relevant to them. After five or six lessons on various topics that explore the intersections of popular culture and social justice, students will have generated poems that demonstrate a high level of critical thinking, but only if there is dialogue surrounding the topics.

In our interview, I asked Eric why he wrote that he gets excited about spoken word, but discouraged by academic essays. He speculates, "I think it's just writing what I believe in, is basically what empowers me." Creating opportunities for students to "write what they believe in" is central to *Word Up!* and Breakbeat Pedagogy. Without personal, relevant writing that values students' convictions, there can be no event. *Word Up!* and Breakbeat Pedagogy are predicated on the assumption that students have something valuable to say and there is an audience that wants to hear them say it.

I Am Here / The Affirmation of Identity

Before getting behind a microphone and voicing their opinions, beliefs, and ideas, students in the Slam Poetry Club had a lot of practice sharing in front of each other. It wasn't uncommon to hear students snapping and cheering in the middle of one another's poems during a workshop session. We created a culture of listening that has its roots in Hip Hop and spoken word culture. The snapping is an affirmation, much like the call-and-response traditions of African American churches and Hip Hop concerts. It is an encouragement to continue in the present moment—an affirmation that "yes, we are here, despite those who try to deny our existence and silence our voice."

Many students, including Eric, have cited the snapping as a motivator that provided courage to share their personal writing. Eric spoke highly of the encouragement he received from his peers in the Slam Poetry Club:

> It helps me to keep going…it's kind of like my motivation in a way. It's like, these people like your writing, so you must be doing something right.

Many times, in traditional English classes, there are no spaces to discover that others "like your writing." Students submit papers to instructors who comment and offer suggestions on revision, but how often do we create authentic spaces for listening, appreciating, and understanding one another's writing? The Slam Poetry Club, as a participatory learning space, is a community of writers who support one another's struggles to name their experiences. In a particularly poignant part of our interview, Eric explains this dynamic:

> **Me:** So I'm wondering why is it important to be in and feel like part of a writing community?
>
> **Eric:** I think it's like a support system…. If you're just like out there alone…writing alone, you never really expand yourself.

Like Eric, I also came to see the community as a support system. I was often taken aback by the therapeutic value of one writer helping another. Of course, it is possible to write in solitude, and perhaps even grow and improve. But Eric talks about expansion here. What does it mean to "expand" as a writer? I think of Walt Whitman's famous line in which he declares, "I am large, I contain multitudes." I make the claim here that writing is a deeply human, profoundly social practice. We need to interact and fill ourselves with the multitudes of other writers in order to grow and expand our possibilities.

Collective Empathy and Healing

The real value of participating in a writing community has a lot to do with empathy, or the capacity to understand one another. When we really listen to someone's story, we will find more similarities than differences if we seek to identify instead of compare. Eric reflects on the role of empathy in the Slam Poetry Club:

> You have no idea what a person has witnessed. You may not like the person, but at least respect their story and try to understand them.

In his midterm exam during the year I had him in class, Eric wrote more about this idea, arguing, "My capacity for empathy has grown through reading and writing." This is evidenced by his writing of persona poems through different voices, such as a prostitute, a cigarette, and various other perspectives that are often overlooked or discarded.

In a memorable commentary, Eric wrote about Papi, the divisive figure in the short story "Fiesta, 1980" by Junot Díaz. Papi, the patriarch of the family, cheats on his wife and abuses his children. Eric was the only student to question Papi's motives, history, and background. While most students dismissed Papi as a purely immoral character, a womanizer, and cheater, Eric insisted on at least striving to understand him:

> I wanted to ask my peers, "Why is Papi the way he is?"…I am not defending Papi, but…we judge him as a "bad guy" when we know nothing of his story. We only see his actions in the confines of a few pages of text.

Eric wondered whether this insight was evidence of his empathy. This suggests that his metacognitive awareness has grown and I wonder how much the Slam Poetry Club and his participation in *Word Up!* are responsible for that growth. Clearly, Eric is a reflective and courageous young man independent of our writing community. However, it seems his participation in a community of writers who encourage active listening and sharing of personal experience has opened him and, indeed, increased his capacity for empathy.

But for me, Eric's most memorable words weren't spoken on stage at *Word Up!* They weren't written in an essay. They can't even be found in his reflective writer self-study. The words that define him most, as a writer, came in response to the following question during our interview:

> **Me:** Who are your favorite writers, poets, or rappers?
>
> **Eric:** My favorite poets would have to be my peers. It's such an honor to see their growth and my growth along with them.

These words will inform my teaching more than any others. These words tell the story of this project and reflect the potential of Breakbeat Pedagogy. These words remind us that to live a life of writing is to experience one another intimately as we grow, struggle, and find our voices together.

The poem that best demonstrates Eric's growing ability to think critically about the world is "Tombstones." He wrote it shortly after the summer of 2014 when police in Ferguson, Missouri, murdered unarmed teenager Mike Brown. Eric performed this poem at *Word Up!* and again at the Louder Than a Bomb poetry festival in Camden, New Jersey.

> **Tombstones**
> by Eric
>
> I don't talk race at the dinner table because if I do,
> all I'll be eating is the garbage that is a regurgitation of these biased news networks.
> We are spoon fed information
> But our minds are the emaciated corpses of facts,
> and all that rise are mindless opinions.

Facts:
Darren Wilson did not file an incident report,
clarity is too hard to digest,
so let's keep truth in suspended animation.
Frozen, mystery, myth,
You got cops that are supposed to find answers.
But why is Mike Brown left as an open-ended question,
open to interpretation, open to opinion,
open to people stuffing unlived memories into his lifeless body.

Darren Wilson, 6'4" stated Mike Brown, 6'4", lunged at him.
Bang.
He said "self defense"
Bang. Bang.
I would've believed him.
Bang. Bang. Bang.

Mr. Wilson, you might have overdone it.
The build of a football player,
but if one hot metal bullet does not have him on the ground
he must be more than a human. But that's just it, he was a human.
The bigger they are the harder they fall.
Let them demonize you for stealing cigarillos
Paint you as a criminal who deserved death
And would amount to nothing but a street corner.

This isn't the first time, people.
Black man is a criminal,
White man is disturbed.
People of color never became champions of law because
America didn't craft it for us.
White people like to take the law into their own hands and use it as the gun to fire.
But when they are invaded by the outcrying marches of inner city brothers and sisters, they use the law as a shield—

"I was doing my job" "He was reaching for a gun" "He was resisting arrest"
I guess that gives you a right to murder promised men.

Emmett was just an innocent boy who found beauty in a white woman, even though her people had oppressed him.

Eric Garner said I CAN'T BREATHE, I CAN'T BREATHE, I CAN'T—

Mike Brown was shot 6 times, 6 times too many

Tamir Rice was having the time of his life until they drove up and ended it.

Oscar Grant, I bet his last thoughts to his daughter were "daddy ain't coming home"

Trayvon was walking with a hoodie on, just walking.

I was raised to believe we lived in a country where all of this had passed, where none of this was possible.
Dear America, why is it possible?

From the start, Eric is already critical of both his family's beliefs and the corporate news media, and he expresses a desire to break free from both. He is critiquing the August 2014 killing of Mike Brown in Ferguson, Missouri, and the failure of the grand jury to indict Officer Darren Wilson, which led to months of protests and clashes between police and demonstrators.

Eric includes specific details from the police report and integrates facts into his poem. This is a skill we try to cultivate in young people, but Eric is doing it here without being prompted. He is invested in this story. As a young person of color, Eric understands what's at stake and refuses to passively consume the dominant narratives perpetuated by the media. He integrates research, personal narrative, poetic language, and current events into a seamless testimony of time and place.

Eric is disturbed by the dehumanization of Mike Brown, who was characterized by the officer as possessing superhuman strength. The officer insisted that Brown posed a threat to him and even went as far as to describe him as a "demon." These descriptions reflect our unwillingness to see the humanity in black men. Eric actually uses the word "demonize" in its traditional sense, which juxtaposes with the disturbing literal use of the word from the police officer.

He expresses the racist double standards of our society as he writes, "Black man is a criminal, / White man is disturbed." This sense of injustice is immediate and relevant. It came to define 2015 for many people, reminding us how far we still have left to go when it comes to racial justice. Eric's poem addresses a specific incident, conjures up old traumas such as that of Emmett Till, and contextualizes all of it from a perspective that is unique to him.

Many would have us believe that racism is a thing of the past, that we live in a post-racial America, and that color blindness is a virtue that shields us from hate. Eric's poem highlights some disturbing truths and contradictions that radically oppose these ideas. His poem is emotional and personal, but also calculated, critical, researched, and political. He does so much of what we want students to do when they write a research paper or study current events. I don't know whether this kind of criticality can be taught, but in a classroom that invites students to process and cultivate their anger, fears, frustrations, and confusions in a healthy way, there is an opportunity for students to develop a sense of critical consciousness. Here lies the power of the Hip Hop and spoken word classroom.

.7.
READING AS BREAKING

Hip hop enthusiasts, crate diggin' analysts / Break beat choppin' / Turntable protagonists
—Phonte

Kendrick Lamar participates in a cypher with students in Brian Mooney's classroom.

Reader as Self

This chapter focuses on an eleventh grade student whom I worked with between 2012 and 2015. Treena (a pseudonym) is a seventeen-year-old African American dance major. She also identifies as a poet or spoken word artist. I met Treena during my first year of teaching and our relationship continued to develop through our work with spoken word poetry. Treena regularly attended the Slam Poetry Club that meets on Tuesdays after school and performed in three *Word Up!* events.

When conducting this case study, we decided to meet in my classroom during a free period. As in my work with Eric, I was transparent with the study, informing Treena of its scope and vision—and sharing an overview of my research. I asked her to complete a Reader Survey (see Appendix I) before our first meeting. This served as a guide to our discussion, which focused for the most part on Treena's love of performance poetry, but also on her dislike of mandated school reading. When asked about her attitudes toward reading, Treena differentiated between in-school and out-of-school reading. She described school as an "institution" where reading for pleasure is unlikely to occur. It's important to note her use of the word "institution." She recognizes the authoritative forces that often dictate curriculum and pedagogy. Our interview was conducted inside the institution, at my desk, a site that can never be free of the institutional powers that she discusses.

Although our interactions in the context of this reader case study occurred at school, I also interacted with Treena outside of school at a poetry slam in Jersey City. I sent home a notice to parents of students who attend the Slam Poetry Club, informing them of this out-of-school event at which I would be present. In order to avoid any conflicts, I informed the assistant principal that I'd be attending an event where some of our students would be performing. Treena was one of them.

Treena is an avid reader. In the Reader Survey, she wrote, "I own a ton of books. There are piles in my mom's basement and in my dad's treasury. I have books sitting by my closet, under my bed and on my Kindle app; but I haven't read most of them." This proximity to books was also common at school in her earlier years. Growing up in North Carolina, Treena recalls that there was "a library at the school and if you read a certain amount of books for that age group then you got a sort of prize or you got to do something very exciting."

She remembers this as a voluntary experience and repeats, "I don't remember this being mandatory." It wasn't until years later that Treena experienced a dislike for reading:

> I remember group-reading times in younger grades and then I remember just reading schoolbooks and textbooks and everything I didn't want to read. And that just made me not want to read anything else.

There are two important shifts that took place in Treena's reading history. First, reading moved from a group activity to an isolated individual activity. Second, the content changed. In her younger years, presumably middle school, Treena had the freedom to choose what books she read. As she got older, textbooks became mandated reading and there was less time for enjoyable, independent reading of her choosing. The result, as Treena expresses, was a loss of interest for reading in general.

Spoken Word Identities

Treena is a dancer. She trains and rehearses for performances with other dance majors in our school's Performing Arts Department. I was curious about how Treena's identity as a dancer intersects with her identity as a reader. I asked her about the similarities between dance and spoken word:

> I kind of experience [dance] like listening to poetry because they [are] both very visual [and] very abstract...and something that you can understand, too. Or something that you can interpret, so that you do understand.... Spoken word specifically, and dance, both involve a performance quality that is very appealing and helps you try to get your point across. If I were to dance kind of solemnly, kind of out of energy, it would be different if I danced with all of me. And the same with poetry. If you just read it, it's one thing. But if you actually put your emphasis on the words and if you give it your energy, it's a different experience.

Treena is a visual and kinesthetic learner. She needs to see, feel, and hear movement in order to understand. She is drawn to the abstract, but also to concrete understandings. Treena is a performer of literacy. Her identity as a dancer is not so different from her identity as a reader and writer. Both acts are performative. They both demand a "showing up," a kind of energetic attention and investment. She describes both dance and spoken word as "experiences." Treena is talking about aesthetics, or the qualities of something. She "reads" abstract concepts, themes, and ideas in bodily movements much like she reads a performance poet embodying meaning through words. This kind of aesthetic education is what Maxine Greene (2001) describes when she speaks about "going out towards" a text in search of understanding.

Although dance has been part of Treena's life for several years, spoken word poetry is a relatively new interest. During the spring of 2013, I assigned a project to my sophomores, including Treena's class. They were to design a poetry anthology (see Appendix E) in several steps:

1. Explore as many poets as possible (classic & modern) (see Appendix F)
2. Compile approximately 10–12 poems that speak to you
3. Identify a common theme(s) and cluster the poems into sections
4. Write a 4–5 page foreword discussing your selection of each poem

I provided a lengthy list of American poets for students to explore, dividing the list into classic and modern. Most of the modern poets are spoken word artists. After some individual conferences with students, I noticed that many of them were watching spoken word artists on YouTube and finding the written versions of these texts for their anthologies. Some students even transcribed poems they couldn't find in printed texts. During a conference with Treena, I suggested spoken word poets I thought she'd enjoy, including Saul Williams, Jeanann Verlee, and Sarah Kay. It wasn't until the end of the year, when presenting these anthologies, that I learned of Treena's newfound love for spoken word.

In our interview, Treena describes this as a time when "I felt like I dipped into this world that isn't *told*…like I'd been slapped with the most honest of things in this world" (emphasis mine). Treena entered a new discourse community, one that she identified with and envisioned herself as becoming part of. She experienced spoken word as a kind of underground collection of voices that are usually silenced in academic institutions. Although many of the poems she chose for her anthology would be considered inappropriate for a high school classroom, I didn't interfere with her selection process. The poetry anthology project allowed her to explore her identity in ways that ask the following:

- *What stories speak to me?*
- *What voices do I want to hear?*
- *Why do certain voices call to me while others do not?*
- *What themes or ideas are relevant to my life right now?*
- *How do these poems express my different identities?*

Treena's identity as a black female is important to this study. Her process of coming to affiliate herself with spoken word poetry reflects some profound truths about her identity as a reader and writer. I asked her about what kinds of issues, topics, or themes she is drawn to when reading (or watching) spoken word poetry, since many twenty-first-century students are engaged in new forms of literacy that depend on speaking and listening as modes of meaning-making (note: before administering the Reading Survey, I told her she might consider watching poets on YouTube as a form of "reading"):

> I'm drawn to the things that bother me most. Like racial issues. Being black. Or any other ethnic problems. Domestic violence bothers me.... I probably just started [writing about race] recently.... We talk a lot about it in history...but I don't feel free talking about that. I get more like defensive and angry. And I start commenting very...or I'm just like ughhh, God, this again!

She goes on to discuss a recent spoken word poem that she watched on YouTube:

> [It] was about two girls. One of them was black and she was talking about the oppression of black people. And then the other one was white. And she was talking about gender. And they were going back and forth talking about how they've both been oppressed, basically. And how, "OK you think your life is hard but mine is like this" and that was a very powerful poem. Because not only did you see the perspective from an African American but you also saw the perspective from the white girl. And they dipped into each other's problems. And they shared them.

Treena doesn't feel comfortable talking about race in history class, but she is drawn to spoken word poetry that confronts it. Our school is diverse, but African Americans are still in the minority and Treena's history teacher is white. Do these factors affect Treena's response to discussions of race in that classroom? Why does she become defensive and angry? How does Treena negotiate her institutional identity (Gee, 2000) as a high school student and her affinity identity as a member of the spoken word community? These questions still linger, but Treena's writing speaks to this process more authentically than my conjectures and shows us a great deal about her identity as a reader, as well.

Before moving on, I want to give my attention to Treena's discussion of the poem she watched on YouTube, as she describes the two women performers who "dipped into each other's problems. And they shared them." What does it mean to share in each other's problems? Do good readers look for the opportunity to do this? I would argue yes. Proficient readers are not just great decoders of words and symbols. I want to argue that great readers look for ways to cultivate empathy. They inhabit voices that are sometimes radically different from their own. They embody these voices in the text. They consider multiple, conflicting perspectives. Treena's capacity for empathy is evident here as she considers not only the race of the African American poet but also the gender of the white poet. She reads through multiple lenses and finds opportunities to identify with two poets who represent two different marginalized, yet intersecting parts of her own identity.

Patsey

Besides my interactions with Treena in school, I've also had the privilege to share some time with her in an out-of-school context. A group of spoken word artists in Jersey City hold regular poetry slams in which poets compete for a spot on their team. The venue is a restaurant in downtown Jersey City. Unlike school, this is a completely uncensored space. Many of the poems deal with adult themes. In this way, it is a site of conflict for me as an educator. I am a different version of my teacher-self in this context, but I'm still their teacher while my students are present. But this situation also offers some great benefits. I get to experience my students in an environment free of many institutional barriers (but of course, not all).

Treena started writing and performing spoken word at our school event, *Word Up!* She returned after the summer of 2013 with new poetry to share with us. She had evolved as a writer and performer, something evident in her writing reproduced here. I argue that Treena's poem "Patsey," inspired by the character in *12 Years a Slave* played by Lupita Nyong'o, who won the 2013 Academy Award for Best Supporting Actress, demonstrates her ability to "read the world" through a critical lens. This poem reflects the transformation of Treena's reader/writer identity in the context of Breakbeat Pedagogy:

Patsey
by Treena

If it were the 21st century you would have been a model.
They would have admired your plum lips and mud colored skin, Patsey.
It is flawless,
Flawless like broken sunsets and rainbows.
Rainbows
Are for Colored girls, and most colored girls are lost in their own skin.
We are searching,

Rolling around under our heaviest organ,
Bumping into dead-ends,
Stuck in our own limbo,
Trying to find a way out of this shame,
But refusing to escape through our wrists.
Patsey,
What is seen in you is more than your cotton picking.
It is the rays that emit from your body; they threaten with love.
They've sucked the hope from you
But had not quite sucked the color from your skin.
I thought they were inseparable.
Or is there still hope for you?
Is that what keeps the brown skin from rejecting your bones?
Tell me, Patsey.
We girls need to know.
We are stuck searching,
Wandering around like confused souls with plum lips and mud colored skin,
Skin that is flawless like broken sunsets and rainbows,
Rainbows that are for Colored girls who don't seem to belong anywhere
Yet are searching for a way to escape their own flawless skin.
But Patsey, we should call it home.

Treena is "reading" the film as a text. She is responding to it. She is talking back to the world that Patsey, a plantation slave, finds herself trapped inside. Treena demonstrates a deep understanding of the social and historical context of slavery and the racism that has shaped our definition of beauty throughout the centuries. Treena is talking back to the institutional forces of slavery, colonialism, colorism, and racism. It's a poem about race and gender and survival, full of questions and harsh truths, but also hope. When asked about the process of writing this piece, Treena responded with this:

> [It] took some time to revise, a few weeks maybe. I saw the movie and fell in love with the costar, Patsey. When I got home I started writing and writing.... I was still obsessed with the character and this idea of self-racism and being forced to hate one's self.

I argue that Treena's investment in spoken word culture actually sanctioned a space for her to speak in this voice. Unlike the frustration she experienced in history class when discussing race, Treena knows that the norms and conventions of spoken word give her the freedom to read and write in a way that is transgressive (hooks, 1994). She describes the culture of spoken word as "an environment that's very warm and very safe [that] kind of opens you up." I hypothesize that spoken word and Hip Hop provided a space for Treena to read and write with a critical consciousness. Her reading experiences on YouTube opened her to these kinds of voices and styles.

Her poem alludes to Ntozake Shange's (1989) choreo-poem, *"for colored girls who have considered suicide / when the rainbow is enuf."* We often teach allusion as a complicated literary device that is only employed by the most expert professional writers, but Treena is doing it here without being prompted. She is weaving together different inspirations and, interestingly enough, the literature she alludes to is a choreo/dance poem, which makes sense given Treena's identity as a dancer. Here we have a young writer pulling images from all around her immediate world, including film and literature, synthesizing these images and ideas into a powerful commentary on race, colorism, and beauty.

Treena's poem "Patsey" was a highlight of the Jersey City poetry slam. She won her first competition with this piece and it advanced her to the semifinals. She didn't win again, but the experience was another leap into a community of writers and performers that welcomed her, even though most were many years older. She was the youngest poet to perform, competing against seasoned veterans of the poetry slam scene.

Reflecting on Treena's process as a reader raises many questions that I want to take up in future research. I'm particularly interested in the identities that Gee (2000) outlines in his work. I want to know more about Treena's "affinity identity" as a spoken word poet from the Hip Hop generation. How does a student actually claim the title of "reader" or "writer"? What makes a student invest in a discourse like Treena did with spoken word? What other opportunities exist for students like Treena who want to continue growing in their craft? I'm also curious about ways to bridge Treena's dance performances with her spoken word readings. Together, we envisioned a hybrid performance full of movement, sound, and words similar to Shange's choreo-poem. Some programs, like First Wave at the University of Wisconsin–Madison, are already incorporating the work of Hip Hop theater.

Moving forward, we came up with a plan to compete in as many poetry slams as possible. We'd like to compete in the Brave New Voices and Louder Than a Bomb competitions at some point in the future. We also agreed to continue exposing each other to as many new writers as possible. Oftentimes, students like Treena put me on to new poets that I've never heard of. When this happens, I'm thrilled. This means they are invested in the culture, oftentimes reading or watching poems outside of school, and that I can continue to learn from them as they teach me what's relevant.

. 8 .
SPEAKING AS BREAKING

Inhale break beats
–Ghostface Killah

Student-poet performs at Word Up! June 2013.

To Speak a True Word

While Chapters 6 and 7 provide an in-depth look at two individual students who have learned within the framework of Breakbeat Pedagogy over an extended period of time, it is difficult to focus solely on them. There are countless other poems, rap verses, and artifacts produced by my students that are worthy of study, reflection, analysis, and interpretation. It is beneficial to explore the complex identities of a few students, but a discussion of *Word Up!* and Breakbeat Pedagogy would be incomplete without a consideration of the four student poems highlighted in this chapter.

Each of these poems was written by a different member of the Slam Poetry Club, some of whom were also enrolled in my Hip Hop Lit class during the past several years. The poems were written at different times in each writer's development. Some of these students identify as writer, poet, MC, and/or spoken word artist. All four of these poems were performed at *Word Up!* before an audience of approximately two hundred people in the Black Box Theater. Prior to performing, each student workshopped his or her poem with peers and received feedback on both writing and performance. Some of the poems were written in response to a prompt, while others were generated without one. All the poems are original.

Each of these poems was also performed at a youth poetry festival called Louder Than a Bomb (LTAB), which originated in Chicago, but is now hosted in other cities around the United States. We participated in LTAB-Camden in April 2014. The festival and competition took place at Rutgers University and featured nearly a dozen high school poetry slam teams from New Jersey. The poems are presented here in their entirety, followed by a discussion and analysis that aims to situate each poem and its author within the framework of Breakbeat Pedagogy.

It was tempting to include only excerpts or passages from each poem for the sake of brevity. However, I made the decision to include the full text of each poem for several reasons. First, the full text preserves the artistic integrity of each piece and provides more context for the reader. Second, I think it's important for each student whose work is included here to say, "My poem is published in a book." Many of these poems are worthy of publication in their own right, independent of this book, but I wanted to honor their voices by including the entire poems. Each of these students helped me grow as a teacher, writer, and researcher. They are more than classroom artifacts. They are people who have impacted my life in profound ways. Lastly, the poems are enjoyable and entertaining for the reader! My hope is that you will return to this section to reflect on everything I may have missed in discussing each poem because there are subtleties and complexities that I know deserve more attention than I was able to give them here. I hope these texts can serve as examples or mentor-texts for the kind of poems you might produce with your students.

Neema

I first met Neema when she was a sophomore. Neema is an African American student of Cape Verdean descent who openly identifies as a lesbian. Our school has a relatively large population of openly gay students. It isn't uncommon to see two boys or girls holding hands in the hallway. Our school is by no means immune from heterosexism and homophobia, but the administration and teachers have done a commendable job at creating a safe atmosphere that promotes respect among students and staff. The Slam Poetry Club welcomes students who identify as lesbian, gay, bisexual, or transgender, and I've had the privilege of teaching many of these students in my classes and extracurricular activities. There is a sufficient need for more research that focuses on LGBT students who participate in Hip Hop and spoken word communities.

While mainstream Hip Hop has historically marginalized the LGBT population, the poetry slam scene has welcomed them. Many of the earliest "slam poets" identify as lesbian, gay, or transgender. This is one of the few notable distinctions between the cultures of Hip Hop and spoken word.

I first noticed Neema when she was holding hands with her girlfriend in the hallway one afternoon. Soon afterward, she reluctantly joined the Slam Poetry Club after one of her friends convinced her to attend one of our weekly open mic sessions. Neema would remain a member of the club for the next three years, performing in nearly every *Word Up!* event, organizing fundraisers, and serving as a stage manager for each show.

The following poem was written and performed in mid-2013, right before New Jersey legalized gay marriage.

Princess Charming
by Neema

I want to marry a girl.
No, I want to marry a woman.

I know you have accommodations for people like me
but who the hell pulls out a ring, gets on one knee and says,
"will you civil union me?"
No.
My love is worth Jesus singing to the tunes of wedding bells.

I remember when I told my mother,
one of the first things she asked was,
"does this mean you wanna wear boy clothes now?"
"No. Mommy I promise,
the only thing I have in common with boys are the girls we drool over."

I remember telling my father and he went silent
because the girl I love and I don't "look" like a lesbian relationship.
Nowhere in the definition of lesbian does it state, "acts like boy."
Nowhere in the definition of lesbian relationship
does is state that one partner is the "male."
There is no male.
That's kinda the point.

There is equality between us because
identity and gender and sexuality are not cut dry like perforated kitchen towels.
They are not black and white.
They bleed rainbows because the sky is light blue
and sometimes pink and orange and gray and purple.
Nature doesn't give a care
because she knows change and Diversity are beautiful,
and the first caterpillar to have turned into a butterfly
must have been like "holy shit guys!"

This is hard for me but my mom taught me to use my voice
even when it shakes.
And I know words hold no volume
unless spoken with conviction.

I am from a tired party of second-class citizens
who refuse to stay in the closet for your comfort-level.
And if it's unnatural,
don't take Medicine when you're sick or make nasty hot pockets.
And if you don't agree, that's lovely,
but I find the world works better when other people are allowed to have donuts
even though I'm on a diet.
And if I am ill, I'm going to start calling in queer to school—

"Hello, this is attendance. How's Neema doing?"
"Oh still gay. She can't stop thinking about boobs again."

I don't know everything but I do know I love my girlfriend
And love speaks louder than volumes we can Comprehend
And maybe humans are the only Creatures that have an issue with homosexuality
because we have such shitty hearing.

So we beg you,
please vote yes
because your yes will echo into more love in this cold world
because your yes will be the intro to the song we'll sing to the children
because your yes will turn into my "I do."

The theater erupted in cheers and applause when Neema first performed this poem. It was one of those moments when I realized that providing kids with a space to tell these stories is perhaps the most important thing we can do in education. Neema tells her story with all kinds of Hip Hop sensibilities, infusing humor, wit, resistance, and confrontation into a powerful social commentary that is funny, personal, and political.

Right away, Neema breaks from the heteronormative patriarchy with her line, "I want to marry a girl." She expresses a desire that is being institutionally denied to her. She is aware of this injustice and uses her voice to break from the assumptions of those who would deny her this right. Her awareness of this issue is politically charged, especially given the context of New Jersey's legalization process. This is the kind of critical literacy that is possible when students are given the freedom to write and share their stories in ways that speak to their immediate experiences. Neema isn't writing from a detached, objective perspective. She is deeply invested in it. When asked about the poems she's written for *Word Up!*, Neema told me, "Every piece that I've done for [the event] has been something that I was feeling in that specific moment."

Her use of the word "accommodations" in the first stanza raises all kinds of questions about schooling. Usually we associate this word with learning and emotional disabilities, but how do we accommodate or fail to accommodate students who identity as members of target groups? What does it mean to "accommodate" and how is it different from accepting and embracing the identities of these students? Neema critiques civil unions as insufficient "accommodations" that treat LGBT people as sick, deficient, incomplete, and unworthy of the full benefits provided by the law to married couples.

When Neema insists her love is worth "Jesus singing to the tunes of wedding bells," she is radically breaking from the shame and fear that have been instilled in us by religious institutions and their blind interpretations. Neema is reclaiming her dignity, integrity, and spiritual wholeness, both for herself and others, following in the footsteps of poets like Andrea Gibson, her favorite writer.

Neema confronts our preconceived notions with her brilliant use of humor. Her commentary represents a definitive breaking from her parents' ideas about homosexuality. However, humor aside, she is "talking back" to all of us in a critical way. She is speaking her truth into existence. When Neema claims that "identity and gender and sexuality are not cut dry like perforated kitchen towels," she is using metaphor to disrupt our essentialized notions of identity, complicating our binary assumptions of gender. Even those who consider themselves allies with the LGBT community sometimes unknowingly enforce expectations that are fixed, static, and immovable. When Neema discusses the caterpillar transforming into the butterfly, she is asking us to look at people's identities as transformational and fluid rather than static and fixed.

Although it seems that her mother doesn't quite understand her, Neema makes sure to acknowledge the good that has been instilled in her when she admits, "This is hard for me but my mom taught me to use my voice / even when it shakes." Just like her favorite poets, Neema knows that breaking from oppression often means disrupting comfort levels. She knows truth is often harsh, rude, and unapologetic. Breakbeat Pedagogy encourages us to create spaces for this kind of radical truth telling.

Near the end of the poem, Neema returns again to the idea that some people still think homosexuality is a kind of moral and physical sickness or deficiency. She wonders whether humans really just have "shitty hearing." When I try to listen, I hear Neema talking about empathy, our willingness to understand. Finally, she ends with a political call to action. New Jersey legalized gay marriage four months later after a decadelong battle in the state's supreme court.

What does it mean to be a good writer? a good poet? a good storyteller? Before she graduated, I asked Neema about performing this poem for the first time on stage. She told me, "I felt amazing after I performed it. I can't even explain how happy I was that day. I was so proud of myself for being so brave and honest on that stage. I think that was the moment I became a Good Poet." Her performance took place within the Hip Hop art space we created. This moment was really a series of moments. It's likely that Neema had already become a "good" writer before she performed, but she began to see herself this way because of her participation in the event. The reception of her poem was empowering, validating, and therapeutic. Neema began to see herself differently afterwards. We mustn't underestimate the importance of young people engaging with listening audiences.

When I met with each of these students near the end of their senior year, I asked them some broader questions about the event itself and what it meant to them. Neema told me that she sees *Word Up!* as her "baby." Reflecting on the Slam Poetry Club's humble beginnings, she remembers, "I was here when the club first started so I'm kind of emotionally invested in it." How do we get students to invest emotionally in something educational? I get frustrated when I hear politicians and policy makers talk about disengagement in schools. I've found that kids will become invested and excited about participating in their own learning if they see themselves as constructors of the experience. The students who participate in *Word Up!* are invested because it's a student-centered event in the truest sense, with minimal interference from teachers and administrators. They get to choose the poems, music, and artwork, literally constructing the event directly from their imagination, bringing it forth into being, open to the school community as a display of their creative brilliance.

When I asked Neema about the Slam Poetry Club and how it has affected her, she said this:

> We created this atmosphere where everyone feels safe and open and able to talk and develop and write and explore different things that we normally wouldn't do in a classroom.... Now I'm at a place where I write well enough to express myself and say the things I want to say, the things no one else is saying. I'm able to put my voice out there. That's something I didn't feel comfortable with a few years ago but now I do.

Finally, I asked Neema why schools should have an event like *Word Up!* Here's what she told me:

> It's important for schools to have an event like this because it allows people who normally wouldn't perform to get a chance to be on stage.... Our thing is a different type of experience because you're not reading from a script or song [but] you're presenting yourself with a story that you created and brought forth, that you're passionate enough about to share with an audience of strangers.

Aaron

Aaron was a sophomore when he joined the Slam Poetry Club. As a performing arts student, he was accustomed to the stage but expressed dissatisfaction with his major. Aaron described feeling disconnected from the other musicians in his program, leading to a sense of isolation and confusion. He loved music and performance, but felt that he somehow didn't fit in. When I interviewed him near the end of his senior year, he shed light on this time of his high school career:

> Before I did poetry I did a lot of music but I just didn't shine in it. And I was around a lot of students who were shining with it and I felt silenced. I was in these shows but I was always the side part. I felt like I wasn't being me. I was just playing a side role....I felt really, really silenced.... But I remember in my sophomore year my friend said, "You found your thing, you found what makes you happy." And that was really powerful. *Word Up!* gave me a home.

It's interesting that even students who are constantly provided with opportunities to be on stage, such as performing arts students, can feel silenced and isolated. We often think of these students as outgoing and confident. In our school, these students usually form strong bonds because they are working closely on different productions such as musicals, plays, and concerts. On the surface they appear confident when it's show time and the lights are shining. But students of every kind can feel silenced and marginalized, even athletes and other outgoing types. I have experienced many different kinds of students who are drawn to the Slam Poetry Club and *Word Up!* We must expand the horizons of who we think these spaces serve.

Aaron goes on to reflect further on his sophomore year when he was struggling to figure out where he belonged:

> I don't think I had much of a voice.... I wasn't doing a whole lot of anything. I was doing really crappy in class and school. When I discovered *Word Up!*, and I discovered I was a poet, it gave me something to do. [School] wasn't just pointless. I had something to write about. I had something to be excited about in the mornings, that I was going to learn and be with people, and be important.

The kind of purpose and direction that Aaron discovered is a common trend that I observed in my field notes and interview transcripts when students talked about finding the Slam Poetry Club and performing in *Word Up!* His process of discovery was a kind of breakthrough, a kind of breaking away from the margins of silence and into the realm of voice and visibility.

Tuesdays became a sacred day for all of us because that's when the Slam Poetry Club met after school, so many of Aaron's feelings about the Hip Hop and the poetry community we created could just have easily come from my mouth. I, too, felt "excited…in the mornings, that I was going to learn and be with people, and be important." If the space was healing and transformative for students, it was equally as powerful for me. Oftentimes, teachers can feel the same sense of mundane pointlessness in their daily work. Like Aaron, I came to rely on the space we created for my own sense of purpose and direction. Breakbeat Pedagogy is for teachers as much as it is for students.

The following poem, written during Aaron's senior year, was performed at both *Word Up!* and the Louder Than a Bomb youth poetry festival in New Jersey.

Boys Will Be Boys
by Aaron

Boys will be charming
boys will be slick
boys will be short hair
boys will be lean
boys will be handsome
boys will be too much Axe deodorant
boys will be picking the teams
boys will be picking on the last boy chosen
last boy chosen will be
the boy called *pussy*

Boys will be six packs
boys will be six packs of beer
boys will be binge drinking
boys will be after cheerleader asses
boys will be black eyes and mouths full of blood
boys will be dangerous
boys will be 'good side'
boys will be confused in the locker room
as to which one they are

Boys will not be lipsticked
boys will not be pretty in that dress
boys will not be pretty
boys will be seasoned and war torn
boys will be tickets to the gun show
boys will bite bullets for their country
boys will not bite their country for turning them into bullets
boys will be dead
boys will be heroes
boys will not cry at each other's funerals

Boys will be stubble
boys will be five o'clock shadow
boys will be shadow
boys will be dark alleyways
boys will be knifepoint
boys will be not asking tonight

Boys will be fathers and whiskey on weekends
Daughters will come home crying
when boys
war torn boys
won't think collateral damage
When the world says she was asking for it
boys will say
Well,

Boys will be boys

The title of Aaron's poem, "Boys Will Be Boys," is also an old saying that is loaded with implications about masculinity, patriarchy, gender expectations, and ultimately, as Aaron makes the connection, rape culture. It's clear that Aaron is thinking deeply about his male privilege and how it is reflected in our culture's assumptions about masculinity and power. Some might consider this a feminist poem, or at least written through a feminist lens, as it critiques the culture of male privilege and domination that is reinforced in the media and in our schools and universities.

Aaron is processing his own understandings of masculinity here. The repetition of "boys will be" is powerful because it mirrors the repetitive cultural definitions of masculinity that constantly reinforce narrow gender parameters. These restrictive definitions of masculinity hurt both men and women. It hurts men because it insists they must conform to rigid standards of masculinity that don't allow for vulnerability and emotion. We can see this play out clearly in Hip Hop culture, with its misogynistic depictions of women in songs and music videos. "Boys will be boys" has served as an excuse for us to look away from our obligation to think more critically about the ways we are hurting women. It almost goes without saying that our hyper-masculine tendencies are hurtful and sometimes deadly. The recent trend of universities failing to discipline, or even investigate, male students accused of rape is evidence of the need for us to think more critically about the old saying that Aaron highlights for us here.

When we say, "Boys will be boys," are we really saying, "Boys will be aggressive and violent"? Are we really saying, "Boys get a pass"? When we look at Hip Hop as a problematic site of contradictions, we can engage students in dialogue about male privilege and hyper-masculinity. Why do rappers use the word "bitch" or "pussy" to denigrate other males, as if it were the ultimate offense? These aren't questions that I try to answer here, but I pose them to demonstrate the kind of dialogue that a poem like this can generate with and among students and teachers. Hip Hop, because of its problematic contradictions, is a site of exploration with unlimited potential.

Aaron is playing with language in powerful ways in this poem. He changes the word "lipstick" to a verb ("lipsticked") and writes, "Boys will not be lipsticked." He invents a new word to describe an experience that he is trying to understand. This is something academics do all the time in journal articles and books. Young writers should also have the opportunity to play with language while they negotiate the uses of that language. The word Aaron chooses to play with is not arbitrary. It is loaded with meaning. The word "lipstick" is associated with femininity, womanhood, and beauty. Changing it to a verb seems almost to position femininity as something that can be applied to one's exterior. We can consider "lipsticking" a metaphor for becoming feminized. Men resist "lipsticking" because of their preconceived notions about gender norms. Aaron is calling these norms into question by highlighting their hypocritical ambiguity.

We must create spaces for students to make sense of the ways they are privileged and oppressed. Aaron is writing a poem that critiques male privilege from the perspective of a male. This is important to think about because some might argue that the only authentic criticism of patriarchal society should come from a female. This might be true in some respects. However, when it comes to young people who are trying to make sense of the world, I think poets like Aaron should be given the space to reflect on their identities, even when those perspectives are matrixes of contradictions, confusions, problems, and good intentions. As long as a young writer like Aaron is aware of his own privilege and how it has shaped his perspective and ability to write and perform this poem, there should be space for it. It's also important to remember that students like Aaron might still be negotiating their own gender identities and that we are seeing it play out through their writing. We must be careful not to silence this process of exploration and discovery, while at the same time engaging students in critical conversations about gender, power, and privilege. After they graduated, I learned that Aaron began identifying as transgender.

Towards the end of their senior year, I asked Aaron about their participation in *Word Up!* and its significance for them within the context of their high school experience. Their response highlights some important aspects of Breakbeat Pedagogy:

> *Word Up!* is as educational as it is counter-educational. It's almost like unlearning. It's definitely a form of unlearning. And also it's just a form of enlightenment. You get to share ideas in a medium that is most central to your identity. Having an event in schools like this gives opportunities for kids to share ideas in ways that no school, no classroom could ever accomplish.

Unlearning something doesn't just mean content, but practices and pedagogies, as well. Breakbeat Pedagogy is counter-educational in the sense that it breaks from the traditional and historical structures of learning that have been predetermined by adults and funneled through a Eurocentric sieve that filters out the voices of our students. The breakbeat event is unpredictable. It's extemporaneous. It's in and of the moment. It rejects the notion that students are unable to design the structures of their own learning. Like Hip Hop itself, the breakbeat event is anti-institutional in that it transgresses many of the oppressive norms that sever our connections to one another. Breakbeat Pedagogy aims to unite us again, mending the fractures that have blinded us to the brilliance of the young people in our schools.

Hadee

Hadee was one of the original members of the Slam Poetry Club. He became a leader on whom we relied and depended. Hadee is a gay male of South Asian descent. Many of his poems deal with race, class, poverty, LGBT issues, gender equity, intersectionality, beauty, and aesthetics. As an architecture major, his design sensibilities translate into brilliant, carefully constructed poems that explore a myriad of contemporary social issues.

As a resident of Jersey City, Hadee witnessed the growing trend of gentrification in his neighborhood. He was also perplexed by the vast educational discrepancies that characterized his time spent as a student in the Jersey City public schools. He looks at these seemingly unrelated experiences as a web of social injustices, enforced by a system that is designed for some people to fail and for others to prosper.

The following poem is a critique of this system. It weaves together social commentary on issues like educational inequity, gentrification, stereotypes, and police-community relations. It is both deeply personal and deeply political.

An Ode to Jersey City
by Hadee

Let me tell you a story about my city, my sanctuary

Third grader, Jersey City classroom
She says,
"I want to be someone you'd see in a history textbook someday."

Forty-seven, Jersey City teacher
And he tells her,
"That's no way to dream.
Don't you get it?
Kids around here don't dream."

You see, us Jersey City kids,
They made us to fail us.
We don't aspire, we don't inspire
We don't make history.

I'm from high school kids like factory workers
Dusty uniforms.
Black polo shirt and khakis.
Knife fights at lunch.
Checking the clock every five minutes.

I'm from gang signs like finger gymnasts.
Fingers twirl on tightropes
Life hanging in the balance
When did streets become circuses?
People wonder why we have gangs here but they cross the street whenever they see a black man on their side.

I'm from never actually paying for public transportation.
They have this one train called the Bayonne Flyer,
And it saves about two minutes by skipping just about all the stops in the hood.
It scares me that our society goes to such great lengths to make sure that white people feel safe.

It scares me even more that white society is so afraid of minorities having as many rights as them.

I'm from the Hipster Invasion
I've seen Hispanic-owned corner stores emptied out by the dozens
And replaced with corporate boutiques
And the city demolishing the projects to build luxury condos.
Why do we call this a first-world country
When we still price people out of their homes?

I'm from limited opportunities.
If you don't live Downtown, good luck.
If your parents don't have a desk job in the city they secretly hate, good luck.
I never understood why they built police stations next to every high school in the hood.
Or why the church bells in my neighborhood don't ring like the ones on the better side of town.
Or why the Jersey City Police Department hasn't had a person of color in a leadership position in seventeen years.

Listen to me
This is bigger than all of us
They made us to fail us
They made us to fail us
And I am tired

I'm from standing on line at the library with eight books stacked above my head.
Librarians like police officers.
Nail polish bullets through her pistol hands
"Put those back, kid. You wouldn't know how to read all those"

I'm from street-corner grocers
From coffee shoppers complaining about the lack of white people working the counters.
From that grey area in between "Black Twitter" and "White Twitter"
From the words "Open Crib" singing louder than the Gospel
From dreams mounting with every mixtape.

I'm from Jersey City, New Jersey,
And as proud as I am of my city,
I can't help but wonder if it was made to fail me.

What does it mean to be a historical actor? someone with agency? someone who participates in the writing of history itself? Hadee positions himself as all of these things—a constructor of reality, a weaver of dreams, of nightmares, of truths. His poem asks us to think about the way education destroys dreams before the dreamer even has an opportunity to dream. When I first heard Hadee's poem "An Ode to Jersey City," I asked myself whether I have been the teacher who discouraged dreamers from dreaming. Whether I have been the librarian, the gatekeeper of knowledge, the enforcer of silence.

When Hadee equates a librarian with a police officer, he's asking us to consider the ways young people are silenced by those in authority. Sometimes it means law enforcement. Sometimes it means the media. Sometimes it means schools. Sometimes it means teachers. Hadee's tribute to his city raises questions about how and why we learn. Our schools are still based on an industrial model of education that is more than a century old. It is predicated on the notion that we learn solely to enter the economy and contribute to the machine of capitalism. We see evidence of this model in the very imagery of schools and classrooms. Bells. Rows. Standardization. Rote learning. This model has unfortunately come to define the educational experience for many students of color in urban schools.

This discrepancy in how we teach America's young people is rooted in politics of race and class. How we learn is entangled with where we learn. Hadee senses this discrepancy and contextualizes it as part of a larger system of inequality that is set up for people of color to fail. When we look at affluent suburban schools in white communities, we see external resources, supports, and stability. The instability that Hadee senses in his schools also manifests in the community through the changing economic landscape of his neighborhood.

Educational inequity and gentrification share many of the same symptoms. Hadee highlights one of these symptoms as fear of black bodies in public spaces. When he insists that "our society goes to such great lengths to make sure that white people feel safe," he is talking about all domains of public life. This could mean the redrawing of neighborhood transit lines or the oppressive and regimented pedagogies that stifle the freedom of students in urban schools. Black life simply isn't valued as much as white life. For Hadee, this means the black neighborhoods, businesses, and schools that surround him.

An ode, though, is a song of praise. Hadee's poem shows us the dichotomy of loving where you come from, but exercising the moral and intellectual courage it takes to expose the harsh truths, to ask the difficult questions, to see the ugly and the beautiful. This courage and thoughtfulness were evident when I interviewed him about his experiences participating in *Word Up!* For

Hadee, *Word Up!* represented a site of stability that stood in stark contrast to the instability and chaos around him:

> *Word Up!* has always been this constant in my life. I think in life it's good to have that. In my life there aren't too many reoccurring constants that continue to surprise me as I go on. So to have something like that, that you can continue to look forward to, really meant all the world to me. Especially as someone who spent his entire life trying to find his voice, it feels good to have a place, not only where I can feel like I found it, but show the world.

Hadee sees the event as a place he can rely on. The Hip Hop art space becomes almost a surrogate home for him. When I think about the event in this way, I think about all the routines, norms, traditions, and procedures that are required to put together an event like *Word Up!* There is a ritualistic nature to the event. Those rituals become ceremonious. This kind of structured stability, this looking forward with expectation, becomes foundational for young people. It provides them with a sense of excitement, anticipation, and purpose that is grounded in Hip Hop.

Later in our interview, Hadee talks more about why schoolwide Hip Hop and spoken word events are important:

> Schools should have an event like *Word Up!* because for the student performing it gives an outlet…and for the audience it gives them something to empathize with. Every time someone performs a poem at *Word Up!*, there's always something in there that you feel like, okay I feel that, I understand that. And it helps us grow closer to each other. What *Word Up!* has done for [our school], it's given us a sense of community, something to unite with.

Hadee's words remind us that performance art spaces can be therapeutic and healing for entire school communities. The empathy he talks about is something perceivable. It can be heard in snaps and cheers. Sometimes it can be heard through absolute silence, as the crowd listens to a student become vulnerable to her own breaking. The Hip Hop event, in its tradition of radical storytelling, opens up prisms of access, allowing us to become part of one another's process for a moment in time.

I end my discussion of Hadee's poem with one final excerpt from my interview with him. Throughout high school, Hadee's best friend was Neema, who during her freshman year struggled with depression and suicidal thoughts. At one point, she considered ending her life. The following year, Hadee wrote a poem for her, but for privacy reasons didn't name her in the poem. Many students knew it was about Neema, but even I was unaware until afterward. Hadee reflects on his performance of the poem at *Word Up!* in front of a sold-out audience:

> I had written a poem for my best friend who was standing right behind me.... I wrote about something that was very personal to both of us, more so to her. When I finished my poem she came up and ran to the middle of the stage and hugged me right then and there, and in that moment everything stopped, and it was just like me hugging my best friend, after me telling her not to commit suicide, was such an uplifting feeling, so gratifying because it makes you realize that poetry isn't just for yourself. Poetry helps everyone around you. When I look back at high school, one of the things I'll remember the most is *Word Up!*

Jamila

The final poem I discuss here is "Out of Many, One" by Jamila, an African American female student who is now a senior. I've had the privilege of working with Jamila since her freshman year and I've watched her grow into one of the most talented writers and performers I've ever taught. Her poems are powerful commentaries on race, gender, and beauty.

The phrase "Out of Many, One" might sound familiar because it is a translation of the Latin phrase *E Pluribus Unum*, found on the back of the penny. It was included in the Great Seal of the United States and was our nation's motto at the time the seal was created. Jamila's piece is a persona poem in the voice of a penny. She wrote it during a persona poetry workshop in which students studied works of poet Patricia Smith and legendary rapper Nas. The lesson asked students to consider the ways writers can inhabit the voices of other people or objects in order to tell a story of importance.

One major focus of the lesson was race. Smith's poem adopts the voice of a Neo-Nazi skinhead, shedding light on the hypocrisy of hate groups, while Nas's song "I Gave You Power" embodies the voice of a gun who is tired of carrying out violence against black people and decides to jam in his owner's hand. Both are powerful examples of personification giving writers enough distance to write about difficult subject matter while considering multiple perspectives. The lesson concluded with a great writing prompt that asked students to write in the voice of an object. This is the kind of lesson that enables students to study Hip Hop and spoken word in a critically engaging way before producing texts of their own. Many students performed these poems at *Word Up!* Because this lesson has been so effective each year, and reflects so much of what is embodied in Breakbeat Pedagogy, I've decided to include the entire lesson, with rationale, in Appendix J.

Jamila's poem is so powerful that I now use it as a mentor-text example when teaching about persona poetry in all my courses. It's important for us to think about the work of our young writers as source material for peers to study. This enforces the idea that our young people are writers and authors producing texts that are worthy of study and inclusion in published anthologies right alongside the texts used more commonly to study the same techniques.

Jamila uses the penny as a metaphor for the African American experience as an essential component of the economy, but one that is often overlooked, discarded, and undervalued. Her poem has many levels of meaning. She is speaking in a multitude of voices at once, employing a breadth of poetic devices to help her tell a uniquely American story of identity, history, and oppression. Her poem functions as a testament to the power of personification in giving writers the distance and perspective to tell difficult stories of pain and suffering, of perseverance and resilience.

Out of Many, One
by Jamila

Out of many, One with copper colored skin bearing a monument on her back
And "Liberty," raised, bold and screaming, on her face,
one whose value was set so low that years were heavy enough to push it below the worthy line,
One dealt blows of self-depreciation with every scratch and scuff.
I am one in the uniform stacks on stacks
that backs the backs of the silvers and greens,
yet the dollar makes em holla'
and me? I'm a penny.

The forgotten currency.
I overcrowd your empty house corners,
clutter the streets and sidewalks,
Hide in the garbage cans and
"waste the space" in your wallets and money jars.
I lay on the ground of backgrounds.
*I go unnoticed *

But I'm a noisemaker,
My community of coins like to clink in communion.
they carry conversation and jangle.

they make music so sweet you reach deep inside your pockets searching for the
promise your ears made to your thoughts.
Instead you find disappointment weighing down your palms.
silver and bronze sound the same but
You count me out of your change as if I didn't make your purchase.

You tell me that I'm obsolete, then toss me into fountains like I'll make your dreams
come true.
I'm tired of this circulation.
those misunderstanding hands,
They all think that sowing me
Will reap them money trees,
That I'd offer my body to be split open and exploited
so they could scatter my seeds far from their inheritance.
This layer of rust is all that keeps me from drowning in this confusion.

I just want to be used or discontinued.
If you tell someone they aren't good enough
enough times they'll start to believe it.

I remind myself: I make up the thousands and millions!
I back the tender of the middle class man all the way to the millionaire!
But neither of them want to associate with me.

Some say money is the root of all evil
And by now my roots have grown wide and thick.
my trees bear bitter fruit.
it branches outstretched and declares:
a penny thrown from great heights can kill.
I am the mastermind of the economy,
The bane of your existence,
You don't work for the dollar,
but for the stacks on stacks that back the hundreds and thousands.
I am the bronze that has inherited the earth,
The most overlooked of uncertain power, cloaked in shades of greens and crèmes.

I'm too cumbersome to count out,
so I'm simplified and forgotten for everyday use.
But from the ground of the backgrounds
my community of coins clink boldly in communion,
my Liberty placed behind me,
permanently screams to remind them
I won't go unnoticed.

This country was literally built by slaves and immigrants. Jamila's poem is a metaphor for her experience as a black woman in a country that likes to forget this. She gives volume to voices of the forgotten, marginalized, and dehumanized. Human dignity does not fluctuate like inflation, our value oscillating between worthy and unworthy because of the times. Human dignity is absolute, unwavering, constant, and objective. Jamila calls us to affirm the value of black lives.

She declares, "My community of coins like to clink in communion," using alliteration to create a sense of musical unity among the oppressed. Her community of coins are many peoples, perhaps black women in particular. This line evokes a sense of solidarity, of unity, of power and resistance. I also like to think of the community of coins as the Slam Poetry Club of which Jamila is a member. We are noisemakers. We don't create random, arbitrary noise, but rather the noise of revolution and change. The breakbeat is a pattern of noise that departs from the traditional structure of music. Just like the breakbeat, the poetry we create disrupts the traditional structure of schooling.

Schools have been organized in ways that prevent collectivism, communion, and unity. We have been isolated from one another for too long—by race, class, gender, sexual identity, age, and ability level. The very notion of individual classrooms has isolated us from one another, compartmentalizing our learning into fixed spaces, disconnected from one another in content and consciousness. Jamila's communion of coins speaks to me as an image of what schools might become if we start looking to young people as resources with unlimited assets who must work and learn together in a spirit of freedom.

Jamila's poem invites us to think about cultural appropriation in new ways when she writes, "You tell me that I'm obsolete, then toss me into fountains like I'll make your dreams come true." What does it mean for a person to be obsolete? to feel obsolete? How do white supremacy and patriarchy enforce the idea that there is no use for some people? This presents a serious moral dilemma. Society tells people of color they are worthless at almost every conceivable juncture, from education to policing, but then celebrates their culture when it comes to entertainment and sports. Jamila uses the fountain as a symbol of this contradiction. It is a site of disposal, but also of magic. In the same breath, we dispose of black bodies as we indulge the magic of black culture.

When Jamila expresses her desire to be "used or discontinued," I think about education again. Perhaps it is time we use the experiences of our students as our most valuable magic and discontinue the oppressive, Eurocentric model of industrialized schooling that is simply inadequate for a twenty-first-century democracy. Jamila insists she "won't go unnoticed." We are responsible for ensuring that our students feel visible, valued, and validated.

. 9 .
PIMPING BUTTERFLIES AND TEACHING STARS

This is the funky outline around a classic breakbeat
—Aesop Rock

To Pimp a Butterfly–*inspired artwork by a freshman student.*

The Master Narrative

Although most of my research focuses on the extracurricular spaces of the Slam Poetry Club and Hip Hop Lit course, I've also integrated the study of Hip Hop into my traditional daytime courses in which I teach freshmen and sophomores. One unit in particular is worth reflecting on in order to demonstrate the ways that Hip Hop and traditional literature can be in conversation with each other in meaningful ways. This chapter is an extended adaptation of a blog post that I wrote in April 2015.

At that time, Kendrick Lamar released his sophomore album, *To Pimp a Butterfly* (2015), while I was in the middle of teaching a unit on Toni Morrison's novel *The Bluest Eye* (1970). My freshmen students were grappling with some big ideas and some really complex language. Framing the unit as an "Anti-Oppression" study, we made special efforts to define and explore the kinds of institutional and internalized racism that manifest in the lives of Morrison's African American characters, particularly the eleven-year-old Pecola Breedlove and her mother, Pauline. We posed questions about oppression and the media. After looking at the Dick and Jane primers that serve as precursors to each chapter, we considered the influence of a "master narrative" that always privileges whiteness.

In the novel, set in the 1940s, the Breedlove family lives in poverty. Their only escape is the silver screen, where they idolize the glamorous stars of the film industry. Given the historical context of the novel, we can assume these actors are white. On the rare occasion that a person of color was cast in a feature film during this period, they would surely occupy a subservient role, playing perhaps a butler or maid. So what happens when the collective voice of society perpetuates whiteness as the standard? What happens when children never see themselves as the superhero? the boss? the damsel in distress? the star? The master narrative tells us that white is good, pure, and clean. Perhaps most destructive of all, though, it says white is beautiful.

Butterflies are beautiful, too—and full of color. Butterflies are so beautiful, they can't be made any more so. They can't be manipulated, exploited, controlled, or confined. So why does America keep trying to do these same things to people of color? Why does America keep trying to pimp the butterfly? Surely we must know by now that the civil rights movement was a metamorphosis from which we emerged into a color-blind, post-racial springtime, shedding the cocoon of Jim Crow, right?

It's 2015 and Kendrick Lamar doesn't think so. His album continues the conversation that Toni Morrison started in 1970. Inspired by the Black Is

Beautiful cultural movement of the previous decade, Morrison offers a devastating critique of white supremacy. *The Bluest Eye* is arguably one of the most powerful novels about racism ever written. It critiques the media's obsession with stars like Shirley Temple and Greta Garbo, revealing the psychological madness that results when a little girl becomes the victim of oppression directed inward. Pecola prays for blue eyes—her only wish—thinking that having blue eyes will make her beautiful. Why wouldn't she? Morrison reminds us that this message is everywhere, including "shops, magazines, newspapers, window signs," and that "all the world had agreed a blue-eyed, yellow-haired, pink-skinned doll was what every girl child treasured" (p. 19).

Pecola Breedlove is the butterfly, still being pimped in 2015, and behind decades of mass incarceration, urban renewal, white flight, and gentrification, she's now a middle-aged woman, hoping for change, hoping for springtime. Luckily, she has a soundtrack in *TPAB*.

The Politics of Redemption

While it's problematic to cast Kendrick as a savior for Hip Hop and black America, it's equally as dangerous to dismiss him. He offers a new brand of hope for the Hip Hop generation, one that is rooted in traditions of resistance and struggle. With pain and anger in his voice on "The Blacker the Berry," Kendrick describes weeping "when Trayvon Martin was in the street." It's easy to become devastated by the stagnation of race relations in America. But Kendrick is careful to balance the chaos with a clear and purposeful sense of direction, even when shining the light on his own hypocritical double consciousness. So how do we help our students find hope amidst such chaos and contradiction?

My freshmen students were devastated when Pecola was raped and impregnated by her own father. Many school districts ban the novel for the graphic writing depicting this scene. However, I'm willing to feel uncomfortable with my students if it means we can reimagine alternative realities for Pecola.

What would have happened if Pecola listened to Kendrick's hit single "i," which celebrates "I love myself" in a world that tells black people not to? Would the outcome of the story, Pecola's schizophrenic break with reality, have played out differently if she heard Rapsody's standout verse on "Complexion (A Zulu Love)," where she raps about self-love? I'm not arguing that music could have prevented Pecola's rape, or that we should assign blame to people who don't know how to love themselves, but perhaps Pecola's blackness could have taken on new meaning and new beauty if she had influences like Kendrick or Rapsody. Perhaps she could have responded more critically to the cacophony of oppressive voices that enforce the master narrative and lead to internalized oppression for too many people. Morrison writes that the marigolds didn't grow that spring. Nothing grew. The soil of that land was polluted, corrupted. It's likely there were no butterflies that year.

When I asked my freshmen students whether they saw any hope in the novel, their response was somewhat problematic. Most saw none. And I don't blame them. The language is beautiful, but the narrative is bleak, dark, and depressing. But it's what we do with our critical reading of the text that matters. It's the honest conversations, reflections, and revised understandings that extend our reading onto the world around us. That's where the promise of hope lives. One of my students, in a commentary response on my class blog, articulated this idea in a powerful way for all of us:

> The novel represents hope because it is somebody taking notice and writing about all this oppression and racism. It brings attention to these serious problems and when people are aware, action follows. Even though Pecola's story ends sadly, more hope is represented in Claudia [the narrator], for she does not totally succumb to the oppression. She pulls apart the [white baby] doll, questioning why it is so beautiful, [and] she has the strength to…pray for Pecola when Pecola is pregnant, planting the marigolds to help, and not judging like the rest of the town.

This is the kind of extended and expanded thinking that we want to elicit from our students. As Linda Christensen (2009) says, we want to teach for "joy and justice," finding the hope in our critical readings and extending those understandings to the world around us. When I think about what it means to practice critical media literacy and what Paulo Freire (1970) calls "critical consciousness," I think about my students looking twice at an advertisement on their newsfeed and asking themselves questions like these:

- *Who made this image?*
- *Who is their intended audience?*
- *What is their agenda?*
- *Whom does this image include? Whom does it not include?*
- *Who has the power in this image? Who doesn't?*
- *What beliefs, values, or ideologies does this image promote?*

Our twenty-first-century students are great consumers. They are saturated with information, media, and layers of subtext. If we don't ask them to critique different kinds of media, to "read" the world through a critical lens, we aren't teaching literacy at all. They must then become producers of new knowledge and new understandings, new texts and new meanings. Breakbeat Pedagogy invites students to move from consumer to producer.

Black Lives Matter

If I pedagogically ignored Kendrick's album release at a time when my students were reading Toni Morrison alongside articles about Mike Brown, Ferguson, #BlackLivesMatter—and considering the disposability of black bodies in an America that constructs a standard of beauty based solely on whiteness—I would have missed an opportunity to engage them in a pivotal conversation about race, hope, and justice. I would have missed an opportunity to speak to their Hip Hop sensibilities—their Hip Hop ways of being and knowing. I would have missed a chance to develop a set of profound connections to a popular culture text that is part of their lives. So here's the first thing I did: As students concluded their reading of the novel, I assigned a Critical Lens Essay that asks them to "look deeply at the text, think for yourself, and consider the kinds of oppression that are experienced by the characters in Morrison's novel." My initial essay prompt looked like this:

> What kinds of oppression do black people experience when the collective voice of society tells them they must adhere to white standards of beauty?

After listening to *To Pimp a Butterfly* and noticing connections to the unit in almost every song, we studied some of the tracks together (which I discuss in a following section) and I created a second, optional prompt to choose from:

> How is the influence of the "Black Is Beautiful" cultural movement of the 1960s visible in both Toni Morrison's novel, *The Bluest Eye* (1970), and Kendrick Lamar's album, *To Pimp A Butterfly* (2015)? Consider the ways both authors comment on how oppression manifests itself as internalized racism.

More than half my students opted for the second prompt, even though it requires more work. They were required to quote from both Morrison's novel and Kendrick's album as evidence and discuss that evidence at length, demonstrating how it proves a carefully constructed thesis statement. I made a pedagogical decision to provide the "edited" or "clean" lyrics to a select group of songs on the album and I even posted a link to the "edited" version on iTunes. I know most students have access to the "explicit" version, and I would have no objections if they quoted from these versions, but since these students are freshmen, some of whom might have parents who object to profanity, even when it's being used for a noble, just, and artistic cause, I decided to give them access to a version without profanity. I find it problematic to call an album like this "dirty." Oftentimes, with some of my older students, and in my after-school Hip Hop Lit extracurricular class, I use the unedited versions of songs to maintain their artistic integrity—or to highlight their blatant violence, misogyny, or sexism.

To Pimp a Curriculum

The politics of Hip Hop education are complex. Students are assigned Vonnegut for summer reading, complete with multiple uses of the word "fuck" and a voyeuristic sexual scene that makes many adults uncomfortable, but we allow this, and in fact require it, because Vonnegut is white. He's been accepted into the literary canon, and thus his writing is considered "high art." Hip Hop is still the subject of intense, misdirected hatred and discrimination in schools. We aren't protecting students from vulgarity when we forbid Hip Hop in the classroom. We are protecting ourselves from our fears about race while simultaneously robbing our students of authentic opportunities to think critically about the media they consume. Literacy in the twenty-first century means bringing many different kinds of "text" into the classroom, especially Hip Hop.

Before I assigned the second writing prompt, we did some close listening to several songs on *TPAB*, specifically looking for Kendrick's commentary on the kinds of oppression we learned about while reading *The Bluest Eye*. The levels of oppression that we focused on most were "internalized" and "institutional" (there's actually a *TPAB* track called "Institutionalized").

The song with the most visible connections to Morrison's novel is the track "Complexion (A Zulu Love)," in which female MC Rapsody confesses that like Pecola, she was "12 years of age, thinkin' [her] shade too dark" and asks the listener, "When did you stop loving the color of your skin, color of your eyes?" In some ways, she's speaking directly to the Pecola Breedloves of 2015, the butterflies who have been pimped into hating themselves.

Rapsody goes on to declare, like Kendrick, "I love myself," and encourages young black women to "keep your head up," because "light don't mean you smart, bein' dark don't make you stupid."

Students pointed out that "Complexion" is about loving your skin tone, which reminded them of a video we watched at the beginning of the unit in which a young woman talked about bleaching her skin to appear more white. Students asked questions about the Zulus and became fascinated with the Zulu resistance to British colonialism, highlighting the counter-narrative that this song offers in response to institutional oppression.

When students listened to "King Kunta," I showed them a clip from *Roots*, in which eighteenth-century slave Kunta Kinte, who became a symbol for "the struggle of all ethnic groups to preserve their cultural heritage"("More About Kunta Kinte"), refuses to adopt the white name of Toby, assigned to him by his white slave-master. I asked students, "Why do you think he's refusing to take the new name?" One student explained that "Kunta" represents his identity—his African identity—"it's like what makes him who he is—and to give that up, is to give up his identity."

After we listened to the track "Institutionalized," one of my students pointed out that her skin was like "an institution" that was keeping her trapped in a predetermined future, much like a correctional facility, hospital, or ghetto. She pointed to textual evidence in the song that suggests Kendrick is really talking about Compton, his hometown, as an institution that keeps people trapped inside it, even after they've left. This led to a discussion about poverty as an institutional construct rather than a personal responsibility.

The last song we analyzed was "u." Students noticed that Kendrick, or the speaker, seems to be talking to himself in the mirror, or at least to his inner demons, contemplating suicide. I asked them how Kendrick's demons are similar to and different from Pecola Breedlove's demons. We considered the references to mental illness, stress, suicide, anxiety, and post-traumatic stress disorder (PTSD) that surface throughout the album. These same kinds of visceral responses to trauma can also be seen in Morrison's novel. After pulling evidence from multiple sources, doing research, and engaging in dialogue, students wrote essays comparing *The Bluest Eye* and *TPAB*.

Breaking at the Seams

Although it would be meaningful to discuss several different student essays, I focus here on one in particular. Jovelyn, a freshman, was one of the students who presented her work when Kendrick visited our school. She was chosen based on the strength of this essay. I feel it demonstrates a great deal about her ability to "read the world" critically. Let's look at several passages from her essay. First, her thesis:

> Both *The Bluest Eye* and *To Pimp a Butterfly* express the African American struggle to adhere to white standards.

Jovelyn's thesis is clear, provable, and debatable. More important, it synthesizes ideas from our discussions about white privilege, the master narrative, and the media's distortion of beauty. She's focusing on two texts, both with strikingly similar themes. She names the oppression. She calls it out. Her thesis is radical, bold, and extraordinarily critical. Jovelyn rewrote her thesis at least ten times as she tried to clarify her thinking and choose language that represented her ideas accurately. In her discussion of textual evidence, she quotes one of Kendrick's songs:

> In the lyrics to "For Sale" Lamar states, "these rappers I came after when they was boring / Lucy gone fill your pockets / Lucy gone move your mama out of Compton / Inside the gigantic mansion…" The lyrics show Kendrick talking to the devil…. Both characters [Pecola Breedlove and Kendrick's persona] are creating little voices in their head because they want to achieve their dreams. Dreams that are both created and crushed by society. They both go through so much that they're starting to rip apart.

She doesn't summarize, but instead offers new insights, using the word "show" to demonstrate that she is making inferences, reading between and beyond the lines of the text. Her comparison of Pecola Breedlove and Kendrick's persona is insightful and provocative. She names "society" as the force that is crushing their dreams. Many readers would cite character flaw, or personal responsibility, as the reason for Pecola's (and perhaps Kendrick's) demise. But Jovelyn looks beyond that simplistic explanation. She senses there are institutional forces at work in the violence perpetrated against people of color. I've wondered how her identity as an Asian American influences this response. In class, Jovelyn acknowledged this identity as a complex one, and in discussions demonstrated a high level of sensitivity to African American oppression. She was always open and willing to discuss the harsh truths about racism in America. Her analysis of another one of Kendrick's songs highlights this critical sensitivity:

> In the lyrics to "For Sale (Interlude)" [a woman's voice] states, "I shouldn't be fucking with you anyway, I need a baller ass, boss ass nigga." This shows that the lady in the

relationship treats the guy as if he was irrelevant because he doesn't have money. These lines demonstrate the belittling of an African American man's character. This couple is a metaphor for how U.S. society treats an African American male. The condescending woman is supposed to represent American society.

Jovelyn's discussion of evidence moves from literal to metaphorical, indicating a high level of critical analysis. She reads beyond the two voices and names them as "U.S. society" and the "African American male." Many readers of this song cannot transcend their own stereotypical thinking. On first listen, it's easy to confuse the woman's superficial attitude as indicative of Kendrick himself, but on closer analysis, it becomes clear that Kendrick is critiquing materialism and capitalism in a way that raises questions about race, self-worth, greed, and exploitation. Jovelyn goes on to discuss the effects of this exploitation:

> [B]oth *The Bluest Eye* (1970) and *To Pimp a Butterfly* (2015) exhibit the insanity and chaos African Americans go through in trying to be a different person.... [When] Pecola's dream of having blue eyes was "granted," it made her insane instead of pretty.

Jovelyn is talking about trauma. She understands that institutional racism is a kind of "insanity and chaos" that can destroy people's humanity. Her analysis echoes Kendrick's references to mental illness, suicidal thoughts, and depression. The symptoms exhibited by Pecola Breedlove and Kendrick Lamar's personas suggest the possibility of PTSD. There is need for further research on the ways that PTSD affects urban youth of color growing up in "harsh worlds," the term Kendrick used to describe Compton during his visit. Sometimes the best we can do is to open up safe, honest spaces for our students to discuss the traumas, anxieties, and stresses that affect them on a daily basis. Finding these connections in literature and popular culture is one way to bring these conversations into the classroom in a healthy way. The price of not creating these spaces is too high.

This Poem Ain't Free
(after Kendrick Lamar's "For Free? Interlude")

What is the price of:
    earth-tone, continent home, soil that don't grow
    off-brand fertilizer in an off-year, no rain, no yams,
    get a receipt with no reparations, subtotal miscalculated,
    tip your local prison warden 20%, please, thank you, chain-gang
    receipt with years of slavery unaccounted for

What is the price of:
> manpower for manhunts for men that escaped plantation
> plantation, sing it, plantation blues, yes,
> amputation, Kunta, Kunta, the MC that moves ya, my left foot can still kick
> your ass, with bars, rap bars, prison bars, prison food,
> leftovers left over to left wing rhetoric, this election ain't freeeeee, you see
> not after captivity
> not after nativity set in white homes in December,
> forty acres and a mule, not forty acres and a pool in the suburbs

What is the price of:
> pensions disappearing like prom dresses
> poverty when it's an individual responsibility
> didn't ya know? jobs become scarce when factories go East
> apologies with no return policy
> pressure so concentrated you can make diamonds
> from the sidewalk cracks in Compton
> dormant giants sleep in the pen tips of public school kids
> whose teachers said, "this curriculum ain't freeeeeee"

What is the price of:
> distorting the news so black boy of 4 says,
> "I'm gonna get me a gun when I'm older"—
> newsflash, cut, news cut, edit out when he says,
> "so I can be a policeman and protect my people"
> porcelain shatter into a thousand shards
> Jesus been picken' up our mess
> making poems out of it
> and he calling his newest chapbook, America

What is the price of:
> this poem, cuz this poem ain't freeeeeeeeee.

. 1 0 .
FUTURE BREAKS

Dear goddess, we made this break beat just for you / As an offering, can you hear us now?
—Saul Williams

Brian Mooney looks on as a guest poet facilitates a writing workshop with students.

It's Bigger Than Hip Hop (–Based Education)

When Kendrick Lamar read an earlier version of the previous chapter, which was first written as a blog post, he contacted me and said that he would like to visit our school. It goes without saying that my students and I were beyond excited. After months of brainstorming, planning, and holding production meetings with colleagues, administrators, and security, we decided to stage a schoolwide event, featuring a panel of scholars, teachers, and students in conversation with Kendrick about his work. Several of the student-poets introduced in this book performed work inspired by *To Pimp a Butterfly* at this event. These poems dealt with topics like race, beauty, and police brutality.

It would have been easy to invite Kendrick to come speak with a small group of students in my classroom, spit some bars, take some pictures, and leave, but we imagined something bigger, potentially more powerful, and accessible to the whole school community. This was a challenge because the only space able to hold the entire student body at one time is the field house, a large warehouse-like building where students take gym classes. This presented a host of logistical problems to solve, but we felt it was worth the effort.

More than anything else, I wanted to make sure the focus of the event was our students and their work. This wasn't a promotional event for Kendrick's music. It wasn't a photo shoot. It wasn't a rap concert. It was an educational event, an opportunity for us to show the world that Hip Hop music can be "literary" and "educational," and that it has the potential to evoke powerful, insightful, critical responses from young people.

For this reason, I wanted to have students perform work inspired by *To Pimp a Butterfly* in order to generate an academic discussion about the educational value of Hip Hop music and culture. I wanted to situate the voices of our students in a larger discourse about education, culture, justice, and hope. To do that, I leaned heavily on a panel discussion format used by an organization called Urban Word NYC.

Every year, for the opening night of their Preemptive Education Conference in New York City, Urban Word pairs a teen poet with a scholar, academic, or community leader. The student performs a poem and the scholar provides a commentary on it. This keeps the student's voice at the center of the event and allows the scholar to contextualize the work, responding in a way that highlights the young person's brilliance, affirms her identity, and shows the rest of us what's possible when this kind of transaction is made possible. I say "transaction" because there's an exchange happening here, much in the same way there is an exchange happening at Hip Hop and spoken word events like *Word Up!* The young person showcases her work, thereby holding it out for us to contemplate and move out toward. The young person receives validation, affirmation, and an opportunity to show us her brilliance from a scholarly platform.

The scholar and those of us in the audience are giving and receiving. We give our attention—not just our intellectual attention, but we listen with our hearts, too. We listen deeply and intently to the young people who are presenting in a forum like this. How often do we *really* listen to young people? How often do we allow them the stages and platforms they deserve? Kendrick Lamar fills stadiums regularly, but our young people are doing work so brilliant that stadiums should be filled for them, too. And if we can't fill a stadium, a school cafeteria will do. A lecture hall will do. An auditorium or gym will do. A field house will do. These forums are created from a place of abundance, not scarcity.

This is what Breakbeat Pedagogy means to me. The Kendrick Lamar event was a major disruption, or break, to the traditional structures of schooling. Class was suspended for the day. Everyone gathered together in the field house, and the entire school community, including teachers, administrators, and the superintendent, was invited to bear witness to a pedagogy that looks beyond the classroom walls. During my short career in this particular school district, it was only the second time the entire school gathered in one place at the same time. This is the potential of Breakbeat Pedagogy. These communal spaces are essential if Hip Hop pedagogies are going to transform schooling. We must find ways to transcend the barriers that isolate us from one another, even within the same building or community.

Circuit Breaks

After reflecting on Kendrick's visit, I began to think about the experience as representing a kind of circuit between teacher-education programs, public schools, and teaching artists.

The panel of discussants consisted of scholars from Teachers College, Columbia University, including my mentor, Dr. Chris Emdin, the leader of the #HipHopEd movement. In addition to Dr. Lyiscott and Kendrick Lamar, we also invited an alumni and our vice principal to participate on the panel. This was a deliberate, careful selection of people. We had two scholars, a classroom teacher, an alumni, an administrator, and an artist. In many ways, this group of people represents an ideal circuit of collaboration for teacher-education programs to consider.

Here's an example. Within teacher-education programs at the academy, teachers (me) learn from scholars and experts (Dr. Emdin) and take that knowledge back to their classrooms to work with students (those who performed) while administrators (our vice principal) are observing, supporting, and guiding teachers who are engaging students with culturally relevant texts produced by contemporary artists (like Kendrick Lamar).

This circuit of teaching and learning involves communication between teacher-education programs, public schools, students, administrators, and artists. We should look to this circuit as a model for what's possible when universities, schools, and artists work together.

Call for Research

While youth poetry festivals like Brave New Voices and Louder Than A Bomb are incredibly important for young people, it's also critical that we think about how individual schools and districts can more fully synthesize the elements of Hip Hop culture within school communities. Louder Than A Bomb starts at the school level, which I think maximizes the impact of Breakbeat Pedagogy, as opposed to festivals that draw only the best and brightest poets from different parts of a region, independent of their school. It's important to support nonprofit organizations and community centers that are willing to do this work independent of the school systems, but there is also a great potential for schools and districts to be transformed from the inside out. I concede there is no shortage of challenges when trying to change the bureaucratic structures that prevent many teachers from doing this work in schools. However, we must continue to transgress. We must continue to put the work on display. It will speak for itself.

More research is needed on school and districtwide Hip Hop events. Many teachers and students want to create these kinds of spaces, but are met with harsh resistance from administrators and thus become silenced. Hip Hop–based education (HHBE) must look beyond the classroom walls if it is to have any lasting impact on school communities. We must create spaces for schools to allow students, teachers, administrators, and members of the wider community to come together in ways that aim to fully synthesize the elements of the culture. Poetry slams, Hip Hop events, and school assemblies that integrate the elements of Hip Hop culture, especially "knowledge of self," are indispensable in moving the conversation about Hip Hop education forward.

The Hip Hop event, as informed by Breakbeat Pedagogy, is a place that might always exist at the margins of schools. As long as there are groups of people who are silenced, marginalized, and oppressed, there will be a need for teachers to create opportunities for those students' voices to be heard. Students who identify as transgender, gay, lesbian, bisexual, or questioning might benefit from the Hip Hop art space if it serves as an authentic forum for radical truth telling, vulnerability, and resistance. All kinds of silenced voices might find validity and affirmation through Hip Hop culture if we are unafraid to ask the difficult questions. There is most definitely a need for more research that explores the relationships between LGBT students and Hip Hop culture. What tensions arise when students identify as LGBT *and* Hip Hop? How do students negotiate these identities? How does the poetry slam or Hip Hop event amplify and/or silence their voices?

We should also think about the increasing number of undocumented immigrants arriving in the United States and how the traditional structures of schooling restrict their access to resources that might improve their lives. How might the use of Hip Hop in schools speak to the experiences of immigrants arriving from Latin America and other parts of the world? What kinds of safe spaces are we creating for these students to tell their stories free of reprisal, in their mother tongues, in spaces that celebrate linguistic diversity and cultural identity? How might the Hip Hop art space take advantage of Hip Hop's global reach among students from different parts of the world? How might we reimagine the Hip Hop art space as an international resource for schools, parents, families, and communities?

As we begin to think beyond the classroom walls, considering global, social, and political contexts, it's important that we return to the community. How can we open the doors of our schools to the small-business owners and local community members who pass by each day? What kinds of opportunities exist for parents and grandparents to feel a sense of belonging and participation inside the schools that their children attend? The Hip Hop art space must be open and accessible. This will raise security concerns, scheduling conflicts, budgeting issues for late buses and transportation, community engagement policy issues, and a slew of other discussions that will and should arise. It's imperative that we break free of the notion that schools exist in isolation from their very surroundings, that somehow schools exist independent of their neighborhoods and local cultures. Breakbeat Pedagogy asks us to reimagine the school building as a site of community. If Hip Hop is the culture of young people, and we have all, teachers included, been affected directly or indirectly by Hip Hop music and culture, then our schools should reflect the impact of this movement, confronting its problematic elements and embracing its healing potential.

We have come to a moment in time when so much is at stake. We might continue subjecting our young people to regimented test-taking pedagogies that serve only the economic interests of the elite and privileged, or we might find the intellectual, emotional, and spiritual courage to break into a different future. This breaking should also be a form of mending and fusing the fractures and divisions that have prevented our schools from becoming democratic sites of freedom, truth, hope. Breakbeat Pedagogy invites us to break from the hegemonic, hyper-capitalistic forces that do not want us to become critically conscious and wide awake to our own becoming. To be in a constant state of becoming is to be in a constant state of breaking. This is the most Hip Hop thing I know.

APPENDIXES

Appendix A

Ten Tips for Teaching Hip Hop and Spoken Word Poetry

1. Be yourself.
If Hip Hop isn't your thing, don't sweat it. Better to "keep it real" and be yourself. In other words, keep it authentic. Find connections to your students that are meaningful to you—but don't be afraid to get out of your comfort zone. If you love classic poetry, boom—spoken word is calling your name. Open your mind to new voices, cultures, perspectives, and ways of seeing the world. Your students need you to!

2. Create open mic time.
My students love reading their poetry during "open mic" time—this is a low-stakes, nonjudgmental period of 10 to 15 minutes at the beginning of every club or class meeting when students can share anything they've written—poems, verses, raps, bars, songs, or short stories. No feedback, just snaps! It's

important to develop a culture of listening and affirmation before getting to this next tip…

3. Workshop the writing.
Start an event! But remember that there is no successful poetry slam or Hip Hop show without good stories. Make sure you spend LOTS of time "workshopping" the poems and songs. Have student-poets and MCs bring in enough copies for everyone and get to work! Emphasize constructive, mature, respectful, critical, specific feedback! This should probably be the number one suggestion! Look at the work of Peter Elbow for incredible writing workshop suggestions.

4. Invite guest poets.
We all know schools have tons of $$$ allocated for MCs and spoken word artists to come visit (yeah, right!)—but you'd be surprised how much $300–$500 can get you, especially if you live near a major city. Do a few bake sales and reach out to your local poets and MCs. Oftentimes, they are looking for work—and having them visit for a workshop and feature performance will do wonders for your students and the school community. I especially recommend Jon Sands!

5. Integrate all of Hip Hop's elements, including its history.
Most people think of Hip Hop as simply rap music. But the MC is just one element of the culture. There's also DJing, Breakdancing, Graffiti Art, and, most important, "Knowledge of Self." If you create a Hip Hop or spoken word event, find ways to get all kinds of students involved in the creation process. Have some kids design artwork and flyers or create a graffiti piece. Others can breakdance in the show. Make one kid the DJ. There's room for everyone!

It's also important to understand that Hip Hop has a complicated social and political history. Understanding Hip Hop as a culture of resistance, born in Jamaica and then transplanted to the South Bronx is essential for doing this work. Teach your students about the socioeconomic conditions that gave birth to Hip Hop in the 1970s, including "urban renewal," the building of the Cross Bronx Expressway, and the resulting "white flight" during a time when the "Bronx was burning" and the world was watching. Jeff Chang's groundbreaking book, *Can't Stop, Won't Stop* (2005), will tell you everything you need to know about the history of the Hip Hop generation.

6. Forget the slam (or don't).

If you're trying to come up with a good structure for your event, forget the slam format! The poetry slam, with its judges and scores, can discourage teenagers who might otherwise rock the mic. Try using a "showcase" format without the judgment. On the other hand, competition can sometimes inspire kids to really write their hearts out. But if your shows get a good turnout and the kids are into it, forget the points—or at least deemphasize them so everyone knows "the points are not the point / the point is the poetry."

7. YouTube is your friend.

There is an enormous archive of performances on YouTube. Use this resource to expose students to many voices and styles—and also to study performance skills. Usually after our "open mic" session, we have a "YouTube featured poet of the week." Let students pick. They usually know who's hot. And for hours upon hours of dopeness, check out my playlist of spoken word poetry that I compiled (disclaimer: some might not be classroom appropriate).

8. Ask your students what's up!

If you want to know which poets or rappers are relevant, ask your students! They put me on to new shit all the time. Get out of the familiar "teacher knows all" comfort zone and let the kids tell YOU what's relevant. Once they know you'll listen, they won't shut up. At all times I have a stack of sticky notes on my desk with names of poets, MCs, and bands for me to check out thanks to my students. This makes me feel cool and young and not pushing thirty.

9. Use existing curriculum.

Until you feel comfortable enough to write your own, use what's out there! *Learn Then Burn* is an awesome spoken word anthology that comes with a teacher guide / workbook companion. Also check out *Toss the Earth: Poems That Move Us*, edited by Geoff Kagan Trenchard, Adam Falkner, and Mahogany L. Browne. It has great poems and even better writing prompts. Lastly, for you Hip Hop educators, check out *Hip Hop Poetry and the Classics* and the newly released *Hip Hop Language Arts*—both amazing curriculums written by Michael Cirelli and Alan Sitomer.

10. Get connected.

There are lots of educators doing this work all over the world. Check out the #HipHopEd Twitter chat on Tuesday nights from 9:00 to 10:00 (EST). We discuss the intersections of Hip Hop, culture, and education while sharing ideas, lesson plans, and a whole lot of resources. Subscribe to Button Poetry on YouTube. They feature incredible poets that you should know about. Lastly, find out if there's a youth organization in your area that promotes literacy among urban youth. Oftentimes these organizations have incredible resources and programs that can support your efforts with Hip Hop and spoken word education. I rely on Urban Word NYC, which also has a location in Los Angeles.

Appendix B

Word Up! **(Sample Format)**

1. Opening Poem—(Student)
2. Introduction (MCs)—(Student, Student, Student)
3. Feature Preview—(Guest Poet)
4. Poem—(Student)
5. Poem—(Student)
6. Poem—(Student)
7. Poem—(Student)
8. Hip Hop Set—(Student)
9. Poem—(Student)
10. Poem—(Student)
11. Poem—(Student)
12. Poem—(Student)
13. Hip Hop Set—(Student)
14. Poem—(Student)
15. Poem—(Student)
16. Poem—(Student)
17. Poem—(Student)
18. Dance Performance—(Student[s])
19. Poem—(Student)
20. Poem—(Student)
21. Poem—(Student)
22. FEATURE—(Guest Poet)—30 min.

Roles & Responsibilities:

MCs: Student, Student, Student
Promotion: EVERYONE!
Social Media Managers: Student, Student, Student
Artwork: Student
Lights: Student
Sound: Student
DJ: Student
Flyers: Student
Tickets: Student
Tickets at the Door: Student, Student, Student
Video: Student
Photos: Student, Student

Appendix C

#HipHopEd Top 40 Educational Value Songs

1. Dead Prez, "They Schools"
2. Nas ft. Lauryn Hill, "If I Ruled the World"
3. Preacher's Delight, "1st First Rap Song" / The Jubilaires, "Preacher and Bear"
4. Blackalicious, "Chemical Calastenics"
5. Public Enemy, "Fight The Power" (full 7-minute version)
6. Queen Latifah, "U.N.I.T.Y."
7. Lauryn Hill, "Mystery of Iniquity"
8. Mos Def, "Mathematics"
9. Mos Def, "Umi Says"
10. The Roots, "What They Do"
11. Nas, "I Can"
12. Queen Latifah ft. Monie Love, "Ladies First"
13. Grandmaster Flash & The Furious Five ft. Mellie Mel, "The Message"
14. Common, "I Used to Love H.E.R."

15. Lupe Fiasco, "Around My Way (Freedom Ain't Free)"
16. Masta Ace, "Beautiful"
17. Kanye West, "Diamonds from Sierra Leone"
18. GZA, "B.I.B.L.E (Basic Instructions Before Leaving Earth)"
19. DJ Jazzy Jeff & Fresh Prince, "Parents Just Don't Understand"
20. Public Enemy, "Burn Hollywood Burn"
21. Yasiin Bey (Mos Def), "New World Water"
22. Dee-1, "My American Dream"
23. Jasiri X, "Trayvon"
24. Gnarls Barkley, "Crazy"
25. Cannibal Ox, "Pigeon"
26. The Roots ft. Monsters of Folk, "Dear God 2.0"
27. Goodie Mob, "Soul Food"
28. KRS 1, "You Must Learn"
29. Big L, "Ebonics"
30. Lupe Fiasco, "American Terrorist"
31. Rapsody ft. Heather Victoria & The Soul Council, "The Drums"
32. Arrested Development, "Living"
33. Kendrick Lamar, "No Make Up"
34. Lauryn Hill, "Everything Is Everything"
35. Wu-Tang Clan, "C.R.E.A.M."
36. Big K.R.I.T., "The Vent"
37. 2Pac, "Keep Ya Head Up"
38. Pete Rock & CL Smooth, "They Reminisce Over You (T.R.O.Y.)"
39. Lauryn Hill, "Doo-Wop (That Thing)"
40. Ice-T, "Colors"

Appendix D
Writing Workshop Guidelines

Workshop Protocol (General Guidelines)

- Respectful, Helpful, Considerate, Caring, Honest, Objective, Mature
- Feedback MUST be specific
- Remember, first drafts are supposed to be crappy!
- There is NO talking during the written feedback portion of the workshop

Workshop Protocol (Written Feedback Guidelines)

- Three specific **Warm** Comments (+)
- Three specific **Cool** Suggestions (−)
- Think about:
    - Figurative Language (metaphors, similes, personification)
    - Sound / Rhythm (alliteration, rhyme, meter)
    - Message / Purpose
    - Abstract / Concrete
    - Fresh Language

Feedback Protocol (see Peter Elbow)

- Sharing (only reading, no feedback)
- Sayback (participants "say back" lines that speak to them)
- Pointing (described above)
- Summarizing
- What's Almost Said or Implied
- Center of Gravity
- Metaphorical Descriptions
    - Describe my piece in terms of weathers, clothing, colors, animals.
    - Describe the shape of my piece. Give me a picture of the reader-writer relationship.
- Analytic Responding (traditional)
- Skeleton Feedback
- Believing and Doubting
- Descriptive Outline
- Movies of the Mind
- Criterion-Based or Judgment-Based Responding

Appendix E

Poetry Anthology Project
(adapted from Dr. Rebecca Packer of New York University)

Purpose and Description:
- Your anthology will be a short book in which collected poems are explored and analyzed in an *Introduction* (or in a *Foreword*), then reprinted with accompanying visuals to highlight both their relationship to one another as well as their significance for you. While the anthologized poems may reflect a single or several themes, they may do so by reflecting a cluster of related issues.
- Remember that you are the editor. No one else has gathered or experienced these poems in just this way. Therefore, the anthology should represent not only the many voices you admire, but also your own vision or personal journey. In other words, your collection is unique. Above all, enjoy the process.

Elements to Be Included:
- **Cover:** to represent your vision for gathering these poems.
- **Table of Contents:** number each page of the Introduction and poems by title and page #.
- **Title:** to represent your concept / theme in gathering these poems.
- **Introduction / Foreword** (4–5 pages): explore and explain the poems' meanings (social, political, and personal), being sure to include the following:
  - *Opening Overview* (1–2 paragraphs): share why these poems are collected together and their overall importance to you—such as their relevance to your journey, your current concern(s), your sense of identity, and/or values.
  - *Introduction of Each Cluster / Group* (1 paragraph each): identify titles of poems and explain how they are related to one another—by theme, style, subject matter, etc.
  - *Exploration of Each Poem* (1 paragraph each): within each cluster / group, analyze poems for deeper meaning and share specific insights into their power / focus, quoting a few lines from text as evidence of your interpretation / understanding.

- *Conclusion* (1–2 paragraphs): share fresh insights into the anthology's poems—their impact on you and their possible value for others. What have you learned about your journey from the process of reading and exploring this collection of poems? Avoid repeating points from the body.
♦ **Poems (8–12):** two may be written by you and/or friends.
♦ **Visuals:** to accompany each individual poem or cluster / group—such as collages, photos, illustrations, graphics, images, etc.
♦ **Aesthetics:** also consider your choices for the following:
  - Type of paper
  - Font, script, calligraphy or pen(wo)manship used to print poems
  - Colors and shapes used
  - Method of presenting poem on the page
  - Method of binding this book together

Final Presentations:
♦ Anthologies are due on the day of your final exam. No late submissions.
♦ Each student will have five minutes to present his/her anthology.
♦ Be prepared to share why / how the anthology reflects your discoveries.
♦ Refer to / quote from a few poems and visuals as evidence of why / how they reflect your journey, vision, and/or current concern(s).
♦ Read a short excerpt from the Introduction / Foreword.
♦ Read a short poem or excerpt from a longer poem.

Common Core State Standards Addressed:
CCSS.ELA-Literacy.RL.9-10.1 Cite strong and thorough textual evidence to support analysis of what the text says explicitly as well as inferences drawn from the text.

CCSS.ELA-Literacy.W.9-10.2 Write informative/explanatory texts to examine and convey complex ideas, concepts, and information clearly and accurately through the effective selection, organization, and analysis of content.

CCSS.ELA-Literacy.W.9-10.3 Write narratives to develop real or imagined experiences or events using effective technique, well-chosen details, and well-structured event sequences.

CCSS.ELA-Literacy.SL.9-10.6 Adapt speech to a variety of contexts and tasks, demonstrating command of formal English when indicated or appropriate.

CCSS.ELA-Literacy.L.9-10.3 Apply knowledge of language to understand how language functions in different contexts, to make effective choices for meaning or style, and to comprehend more fully when reading or listening.

CCSS.ELA-Literacy.L.9-10.5. A Interpret figures of speech (e.g., euphemism, oxymoron) in context and analyze their role in the text.

CCSS.ELA-Literacy.L.9-10.5 Demonstrate understanding of figurative language, word relationships, and nuances in word meanings.

Appendix F

Suggested Poets and MCs

MCs / Rappers

2Pac
Arrested Development
A Tribe Called Quest
Chance the Rapper
Common
De La Soul
Dead Prez
Digable Planets
Goodie Mob
Grandmaster Flash & The Furious Five
GZA
J. Cole
Jasiri X
Jay-Z
Kanye West
Kendrick Lamar
KRS-One
Lauryn Hill
Lupe Fiasco

Macklemore
Mos Def
N.W.A.
Nas
Outkast
Public Enemy
Queen Latifah
Rapsody
The Fugees
The Roots

Poets

Aaron Smith
Aja Monet
Amiri Baraka
Andrea Gibson
Angel Nafis
Anis Mojgani
Aracelis Girmay
Audre Lorde
Aziza Barnes
Buddy Wakefield
Cristin O'Keefe Aptowicz
Crystal Valentine
Danez Smith
Derrick Brown
Erica Miriam Fabri
Etheridge Knight
Gwendolyn Brooks
Idris Goodwin
Jeanann Verlee
Jeffrey McDaniel
John Murillo
Jon Sands
Ken Arkind
Kevin Coval
Lemon Andersen

Mahogany L. Browne
Megan Falley
Michael Cirelli
Mike McGee
Mindy Nettifee
Nate Marshal
Neil Hilborn
Ocean Vuong
Patricia Smith
Patrick Rosal
Phil Kaye
Rachel McKibbens
Rita Dove
Roger Bonair-Agard
Ross Gay
Sarah Kay
Saul Williams
Sekou Sundiata
Shane Koyczan
Taylor Mali
Walt Whitman
Willie Perdomo

Appendix G

Hip Hop Lit Final Exam Writing Assignment

Imagine that the Board of Education is facing budget cuts. They need to eliminate some classes from the curriculum and Hip Hop Lit is being considered. Some of the board members don't think that Hip Hop belongs in school.

TASK:

Write a one-page essay that argues for the inclusion of Hip Hop Lit in next year's curriculum. You should develop a well-crafted argument that relies on specific evidence, such as learning experiences from class this year.

- *How is Hip Hop educational?*
- *How can Hip Hop make us better critical thinkers?*
- *How can Hip Hop serve as a platform for exploring social issues?*
- *What lessons or activities were especially memorable, powerful, or engaging this year?*
- *Why is Hip Hop often conceived as violent, homophobic, and misogynistic? How does our class challenge these assumptions?*
- *How could you describe Hip Hop Lit as a learning community?*
- *What have you learned in this class?*

Appendix H

Writer Self-Study
(adapted from Nicole Callahan of Teachers College, Columbia University)

I'm asking you to complete a kind of mini-writer study on yourself as a writer. Your study is a personal exploration and self-reflection about how people write, learn to write, and improve writing skills. The questions about what to include are suggestions more than requirements. Feel free to include things that are not listed here, and if something feels redundant, don't hold yourself to the form below.

In your self-study, please address the following questions. Please work on them in this order, but if something else comes up as you think and write, feel free to move off on a tangent and then come back to the next question as you are ready. There is no length requirement for this assignment—it should be as long as you need to fully engage in each of these questions.

1. Why do people write?
2. What makes a person a writer / poet / MC? What do you have to do/make/achieve/etc. in order to "earn" that identity or title?
3. What does someone have to do in order to be a *good* writer / poet / MC?
4. Who are your favorite writers / poets / MCs? What do you like about them?
5. Do you consider yourself a writer / poet / MC? Do you consider yourself a *good* writer / poet / MC? Is "writer" or "good writer" a part of your identity? Why or why not?
6. How did you learn to write (poetry, spoken word, raps, freestyles)?
7. Who were you, as a writer, before Slam Poetry Club / Hip Hop Lit / *Word Up!* started? Prolific? Blocked? Passionate? Explain.
8. Who are you, as a writer, now? Prolific? Blocked? Passionate? Explain.
9. What would you like to do better as a writer / poet / MC / performer?
10. Choose a recent piece of writing (perhaps it is a poem you performed at *Word Up!*), but it can be any piece that involved some serious writing and thinking and revising). Read it over with a critical eye, and reflect on your process, skills, and struggles as you created it. What

was the writing experience like for you? Perform a kind of analysis of the writing. What strategies did you employ? Were they effective? What difficulties and obstacles did you encounter in the composition/revision of the piece? How did you feel when it was "published" (performed at *Word Up!*, finished, shared with a friend, workshopped in class, however this piece was sent out into the world)?

11. What kinds of writing do you choose to do? What kinds of writing do you enjoy? What kinds of writing are you required to do? What kinds of writing do you fear? Why?
12. Just quickly reflect on this short experience: What did I gain? What did I learn about my own approach to writing? Was this process painful? fun? exciting? scary? How have I grown as a writer / performer / poet / MC since participating in Slam Poetry Club, Hip Hop Lit, or *Word Up!*?
13. Please attach a poem / rap / piece of writing that bests represents you as a writer (this could be a poem that you performed at *Word Up!* or produced in Slam Poetry Club / Hip Hop Lit).

Appendix I

Reader Self-Study
(adapted from Nicole Callahan of Teachers College, Columbia University)

I'm asking you to complete a kind of mini-reader study on yourself as a reader. Your study is a personal exploration and self-reflection about how people read, learn to read, and improve reading skills. The questions about what to include are suggestions more than requirements. Feel free to include things that are not listed here, and if something feels redundant, don't hold yourself to the form below.

In your self-study, please address the following questions. Please work on them in this order, but if something else comes up as you think and write, feel free to move off on a tangent and then come back to the next question as you are ready. There is no length requirement for this assignment—it should be as long as you need to fully engage in each of these questions.

1. How did you learn to read?
2. Why do people read? What gets people excited about reading? frustrated with reading?
3. What kinds of books / literature do you like to read? (Watching YouTube videos of poets counts as reading.)
4. How many books would you say you own? What kinds?
5. Have you ever re-read a book or re-watched a poem? Why did you re-read it? If so, can you name it/them?
6. Do you ever read books / watch poems at home for pleasure? If so, how often do you read at home for pleasure?
7. How do you decide which books you'll read? which poems you'll watch?
8. Do you have any favorite books? favorite poems? Why are they favorites?
9. What does someone have to do in order to be a good reader?
10. Do you think you are a good reader? Why?
11. What would you like to do better as a reader?
12. In general, how do you feel about reading?

Appendix J

Lesson Plan and Description

The Power of Persona:
Exploring Multiple Perspectives through Hip Hop & Spoken Word Poetry

Literacy in the twenty-first century means equipping students with tools to engage more critically with media and popular culture. Young people need opportunities to become more critical meaning makers as they move from passive consumers to active producers of new texts and media. Hip Hop and spoken word poetry are forms of media that present a culturally relevant opportunity to do just that.

Hip Hop, born in the South Bronx in the 1970s, is the biggest youth movement of the past forty years. It has influenced every facet of youth culture, including music, poetry, dance, visual art, fashion, television, and film. Spoken word or "slam poetry" is a contemporary poetry movement that is closely related to Hip Hop. Many young people, especially students of color, are engaged in elements of Hip Hop culture outside of school. Hip Hop is a fundamental part of their identity.

This lesson asks students to look closely at one spoken word poem and one Hip Hop song before writing a performance piece of their own. Both "mentor texts" deal with inequality, as well as individual and structural racism, through effective use of persona.

Patricia Smith's poem "Skinhead" assumes the voice of a Neo-Nazi skinhead who is presumably incarcerated for perpetrating hate crimes. Smith, an African American woman, is an expert at using persona to shed light on radical, uncomfortable perspectives. Her poem challenges students to think about the ideologies that give rise to hate groups and how individuals may come to identify with them. As a black woman, Smith occupies some of the very social positions that the subject of her poem despises and hates, which makes her attempt to assume his voice that much more powerful. A bold condemnation of racism, ethnocentrism, and hatred, Smith's poem somehow invites us to step momentarily into the mind of white supremacy, shining a disturbing light on all its ugliness and hypocrisy.

In the song "I Gave You Power," rapper Nas takes on the voice of a gun who is tired of killing and decides to jam in its owner's hand. Instead of glorifying violence, Nas asks us to think more deeply about why it happens, speaking in the voice of the gun itself. Incredibly, Nas also uses the gun as a metaphor for African Americans. We see the gun moved from place to place, against its will, struggling to preserve an identity when its serial number is scratched off. Students will begin to see the gun's movement and lack of agency as a metaphor for the African diaspora. This text invites students to think about the long history of oppression and dehumanization that has been inflicted on people of color in the United States, and how that history affects the present moment, especially in the consciousness of black Americans.

These two texts, one in the voice of a person, the other in the voice of an object, serve as powerful examples of personification and how it can be used to approach difficult or uncomfortable subject matter. *Persona* is derived from the Greek word for "mask." This kind of distance provides a degree of safety for students to speak in a voice not necessarily their own, allowing them to get outside of themselves and consider someone else's perspective.

When writing persona poems with young people, I have observed students almost always telling us parts of their *own* stories even when writing in the voice of someone or something else. For example, Jamila's poem "Out of Many, One" is written in the voice of a penny (see Chapter 8). She talked about being "the forgotten currency," but the one who built this country. She talks about her "copper colored skin" and the way she is "toss[ed] into fountains" and forgotten, and about how she also built the economy.

Her poem is personal, but also a social, political, and historical commentary on race, black beauty, oppression, and inequality, told entirely through the voice of an object we frequently overlook: a penny. This is the power of persona in giving students the space and distance to speak their truth to power, gain access to alternate perspectives, and exhibit empathy in their efforts to see through new eyes.

The following lesson provides two powerful examples of persona poems that deal with racial inequality, as well as a writing exercise that asks students to produce a persona poem or rap of their own, with the intention to develop that poem into a performance piece for a schoolwide poetry slam or Hip Hop event.

Lesson Plan

The Power of Persona:
Exploring Multiple Perspectives through Hip Hop & Spoken Word Poetry

Line of Inquiry: *How does personification provide readers and writers with an opportunity to explore perspectives we might not otherwise consider?*

I. **Context**

This lesson asks students to consider the ways two different African American writers provide commentary on racism, inequality, and oppression through effective use of personification. The first text is "Skinhead," by spoken word poet Patricia Smith, and the second is "I Gave You Power," by legendary rapper Nas. Prior to this lesson, students will have engaged in months of community-building exercises, creative writing, and identity work in order to establish a safe space for personal storytelling. Students will have already studied a considerable range of Hip Hop, spoken word, and popular culture texts that comment on different social justice issues related to race, class, gender, sexual identity, ability, and more. Having reflected on our own intersecting identities and thinking about the ways we are privileged in some areas and oppressed in others, students will be ready to begin writing their own performance poems and raps, using persona as a way to safely approach difficult and personal subject matter in a critical and engaging way. The intention is for students to use both of these texts as "mentor texts" and then write their own spoken word or Hip Hop persona poem to be performed at our schoolwide poetry slam known as *Word Up!*

II. **Learning Goals**
   Students will be able to:

   a. Affirm their own identities through performative storytelling.
   b. Exhibit empathy by seeking to understand multiple perspectives.
   c. Explain why authors use figurative language such as personification.
   d. Utilize critical media literacy skills to find meaning in two texts.
   e. Write a poem or rap that employs complex figurative language.

III. Rationale

Students are often the experts when it comes to Hip Hop and spoken word. This knowledge is a valuable asset in the classroom. I chose "Skinhead" by Patricia Smith and "I Gave You Power" by Nas because students are captivated by these two particular performances, which address relevant topics in a critically engaging way.

It's also important to champion African American authors in our classrooms to combat the typically Eurocentric canon of literature that dominates the curriculum. The writers, authors, and artists studied should reflect the diversity of our student populations.

Hip Hop and spoken word use sound and language in ways that are complicated and complex, but recognizable to young people. Most rappers and poets are skilled at combining vernacular and standard dialects. Both of these texts use and manipulate language in ways that are identifiable to students, including elements of African American Vernacular English (AAVE).

This lesson is multimodal and differentiated in that it combines a range of media, including audio, video, and traditional text in order to meet the needs of students with various learning styles. The final writing prompt is further differentiated because it allows students to experiment with personification at various levels of complexity.

IV. Materials

- "Skinhead," by Patricia Smith (YouTube)
- "I Gave You Power," by Nas (YouTube)
- Persona Poetry Handout
- Projector
- Speakers
- Paper & Pens

V. Common Core Standards

   a. CCSS.ELA-LITERACY.RL.9-10.1: Cite strong and thorough textual evidence to support analysis of what the text says explicitly as well as inferences drawn from the text.
   b. CCSS.ELA-LITERACY.RL.7.4: Determine the meaning of words and phrases as they are used in a text, including figurative and connotative meanings; analyze the impact of rhymes and other repetitions

of sounds (e.g., alliteration) on a specific verse or stanza of a poem or section of a story or drama.
c. CCSS.ELA-LITERACY.W.9-10.3: Write narratives to develop real or imagined experiences or events using effective technique, well-chosen details, and well-structured event sequences.
d. CCSS.ELA-LITERACY.SL.9-10.1.D: Respond thoughtfully to diverse perspectives, summarize points of agreement and disagreement, and, when warranted, qualify or justify their own views and understanding and make new connections in light of the evidence and reasoning presented.
e. CCSS.ELA-LITERACY.L.9-10.5: Demonstrate understanding of figurative language, word relationships, and nuances in word meanings.
f. CCSS.ELA-LITERACY.L.9-10.5.A: Interpret figures of speech (e.g., euphemism, oxymoron) in context and analyze their role in the text.

VI. Lesson Sequence
Warm-Up (5 min):

1) Find one object in the room and free-write in its voice.
   a. *What does the object do / think when no one is looking?*
   b. *What does the object want?*
   c. *What does the object fear?*
   d. *What does the object wish people knew?*

Turn & Talk (2 min):

2) Share two or three lines from your free-write with a partner.

Mini-Lesson (8 min):

3) Define "personification."
4) Group reading of "Persona Poetry" handout.
   a. *Why is it helpful sometimes to wear a mask when writing?*
   b. *What does it mean to be vulnerable? as a writer?*
   c. *How does "writing about the self reveal the other" and "writing about the other reveal the self"?*
   d. *Why is it important to get outside of our comfort zone?*

e. How does Smith use "the bag lady" on the subway to demonstrate "how close we all are"?

f. What does Smith mean when she says we should all "get outside of ourselves" in a perfect world?

Close-Listening, Annotation, and Discussion (20 min)

5) Distribute hard copies of each text.
6) Students will be instructed to annotate each text while listening closely. It's helpful to remind students to circle words or references they don't know, underline important ideas, and write in the margins. Educators may choose to play each piece and discuss separately, or play each and discuss both together.
7) Play "Skinhead," by Patricia Smith
8) Play "I Gave You Power," by Nas
9) Discuss / Reflect

   a. Why does the speaker in Smith's poem tell us he has his "own beauty"? Does Smith want us to see him as beautiful?

   b. What kind of room is a "dim matchbox"? Describe it.

   c. Why does the speaker use the words "righteous" and "anointed" and "pure"?

   d. Does the speaker appear confident or insecure? Explain.

   e. What specific groups of people does the speaker hate?

   f. Why is it important to consider the difference between the speaker's identity and Smith's identity as a black woman?

   g. How could a writer put him- or herself in the shoes of someone so different?

   h. Why does the speaker insist, "I'm your baby America…I was born and raised right here"?

   i. Why might Nas, as a rapper, feel used and exploited by the music industry? Who controls the music industry?

   j. How many different places is the gun moved to in the first verse? What do you think it feels like to be moved around so much? What groups of people have been moved around against their will in our country's history?

   k. Why does the gun cite Ohio and Little Rock as places he's lived? How are those places different from Canarsie?

   l. How does the gun feel about killing?

m. What's the significance of the defaced serial number on the other gun? Where do people receive numbers for identification purposes?
n. What does the gun plan to do the next time it's used?
o. Why does the gun say, "my creation was for blacks to kill blacks"?
p. Why do people cite "black-on-black" crime in response to members of the #BlackLivesMatter movement who are protesting the police killings of unarmed black people?
q. How does the end of the song imply that this cycle of violence will continue happening? How can it be stopped? Who's responsibility is it?

Writing Exercise (20 min)

10) Using the prompt provided on the Persona Poetry Handout (and below), students will write a poem or rap using personification.

Step 1: Write down...

- One object you wouldn't pick up if you saw it on the ground.
- One object that holds something you care about inside it.
- One object that you depend on.
- One object that you are afraid of.
- One object on your person at this moment.
- One object you would want to pass on to a child or relative.

Step 2: Now pick the most meaningful one. This will be the object you are writing from the perspective of now, but save the others.

Step 3: Now write down...

- Three words this object would use to describe its owner/user.
- Three things the object wants.
- Three things it does when no one is looking.
- Something you have in common with it.
- Something it is proud of.
- Something it is ashamed of.
- One thing it can't live without.
- The way it wants to die.
- The reward it deserves.

Step 4: Now write in the voice of this object. Tell me about your average day. Tell me about an exceptional day. Talk about the world around you.

Open Mic / Share (15 min)

11) Students share their poems in an open mic format. *It's important to encourage active listening. I always remind students to snap when they hear a line they really like. This helps affirm the writer and keeps the listeners engaged.*

Lesson Extension

12) Following a lesson like this, students would bring their poems to a student-run writing workshop in order to receive feedback. After further revision, students would produce a final two- or three-minute version of the piece and perform it at our school's Hip Hop and spoken word poetry event, *Word Up!*

VII. **Assessment**

    a. Were students able to identify personification in the text?
    b. Were students able to articulate why personification is effective?
    c. Were students able to craft their own poems using effective personification?
    d. Were students able to exhibit empathy when considering multiple perspectives?

REFERENCES

Alim, H. S. (2004). Hearing what's not said and missing what is: Black language in white public space. In C. Paulston & S. Keisling (Eds.), *Discourse and intercultural communication: The essential readings* (pp. 180–197). Malden, MA: Blackwell.

Alim, H. S. (2007). Critical hip hop language pedagogies: Combat, consciousness, and the cultural politics of communication. *Journal of Language, Identity, and Education, 6*(2), 161–176.

American Psychological Association. (2012). Facing the school dropout dilemma. Retrieved from http://www.apa.org/pi/families/resources/school-dropout-prevention.aspx.

Aptowicz, C. (2007). *Words in your face: A guided tour through twenty years of the New York City poetry slam*. Berkeley, CA: Soft Skull Press.

Baldwin, J. (1993). *The fire next time*. New York: Vintage International.

Ball, A. F., & Ellis, P. (2010). Identity and the writing of culturally and linguistically diverse students. In C. Bazerman (Ed.), *Handbook of research on writing* (pp. 225–228). New York, NY: Routledge.

Blau, S. 2003. Performative literacy: The habits of mind of highly literate readers. *Voices From the Middle, 10*(3), 18–22.

Boal, A. (1985). *Theatre of the oppressed*. New York, NY: Theatre Communications Group.

Bourdieu, P., & Passeron, J. (1977). *Reproduction in education, society, and culture*. R. Nice (Trans.). London, England: Sage.

Camangian, P. (2008). Untempered tongues: Teaching performance poetry for social justice. *English Teaching: Practice and Critique, 7*(2), 35–55.

Chandler, P., & Sweller, J. (1991). Cognitive load theory and the format of instruction. *Cognition and Instruction*, 8, 293–332.

Chang, J. (2005). *Can't stop, won't stop: A history of the hip hop generation*. New York, NY: St. Martin's Press.

Christensen, L. (2009). *Teaching for joy and justice: Re-imagining the language arts curriculum*. Milwaukee, WI: Rethinking Schools.

Collins, B. (1988). Introduction to poetry. In *The apple that astonished Paris*. Fayetteville: University of Arkansas Press.

Coval, K., Lansana, Q., & Marshall, N. (Eds.). (2015). *The breakbeat poets: New American poets in the age of hip-hop*. Chicago, IL: Haymarket Books.

Dimitriadis, G. (2001). *Performing identity / performing culture: Hip hop as text, pedagogy, and lived practice*. New York, NY: Peter Lang.

Dunlevy, T. (2000, May 12). The colour barrier is no more. So whose music is it anyway? *Montreal Gazette*, p. A1.

Elbow, P. (1973). *Writing without teachers*. London, England: Oxford University Press.

Elbow, P. (2011). *Vernacular eloquence: What speech can bring to writing*. Oxford, England: Oxford University Press.

Emdin, C. (2010). *Urban science education for the hip hop generation*. Rotterdam, the Netherlands: Sense.

Emdin, C. (2016). *For white folks who teach in the hood...and the rest of ya'll too: Reality pedagogy and urban education*. Boston, MA: Beacon Press.

Fisher, M. T. (2005). From the coffee house to the school house: The promise and potential of spoken word poetry in school contexts. *English Education*, 37(2), 115–131.

Fisher, M. T. (2007). *Writing in rhythm: Spoken word poetry in urban classrooms*. New York, NY: Teachers College Press.

Freire, P. (1970). *Pedagogy of the oppressed*. New York, NY: Continuum.

Freire, P., & Macedo, D. P. (1987). *Literacy: Reading the word & the world*. South Hadley, MA: Bergin & Garvey.

Gee, J. P. (2000). Identity as an analytic lens for research in education. *Review of Research in Education*, 25, 99–125. doi:10.2307/1167322.

Gentry, K. (2012). American visions: Hip hop culture and contemporary literature course syllabus. Retrieved from https://wiki.geneseo.edu/download/attachments/77203195/ENGL%20237%20Gentry%20Sp12%20syllabus.docx?api=v2.

Greene, M. (1995). *Releasing the imagination: Essays on education, the arts, and social change*. San Francisco, CA: Jossey-Bass.

Greene, M., & Lincoln Center Institute. (2001). *Variations on a blue guitar: The Lincoln Center Institute lectures on aesthetic education*. New York, NY: Teachers College Press.

Hill, M. L. (2009). *Beats, rhymes, and classroom life: Hip hop pedagogy and the politics of identity*. New York, NY: Teachers College Press.

hooks, b. (1994). *Teaching to transgress: Education as the practice of freedom*. New York, NY: Routledge.

Hurt, B. (Producer & Director). (2006). *Hip-hop: Beyond beats and rhymes* [Motion picture]. United States: God Bless the Child Productions.

Ignatiev, N. (1995). *How the Irish became white*. New York, NY: Routledge.
Lamar, K. (2015). *To pimp a butterfly* [CD]. Los Angeles, CA: Interscope. Aftermath. Top Dawg Entertainment.
Lamott, A. (1994). *Bird by bird: Some instructions on writing and life*. New York, NY: Pantheon Books.
Larew, J. (1991, June 10–15). Why are droves of unqualified, unprepared kids getting into our top colleges? Because their dads are alumni. *The Washington Monthly*.
Low, B. E. (2011). *Slam school: Learning through conflict in the hip hop and spoken word classroom*. Stanford, CA: Stanford University Press.
Malcolm X, & Haley, A. (1965). *The autobiography of Malcolm X*. New York, NY: Grove Press.
McIntosh, P. (1988). White privilege: Unpacking the invisible knapsack. *Race, Class, and Gender in the United States: An Integrated Study, 4*, 165–169.
McQueen, S. (Director); Ridley, J., & Northup, S. (Writers). (2014). *12 years a slave* [DVD]. United States: Twentieth Century Fox Home Entertainment.
Moffett, J. (1989). *Bridges: From personal writing to the formal essay*. Berkeley, CA: Center for the Study of Writing.
More About Kunta Kinte. (n.d.). Retrieved March 30, 2016, from http://www.kuntakinte.org/history.html.
Morrell, E., Dueñas, R., Garcia, V., & López, J. (2013). *Critical media pedagogy: Teaching for achievement in city schools*. New York, NY: Teachers College Press.
Morrell, E., & Duncan-Andrade, J. (2002). Promoting academic literacy with urban youth through engaging hip hop culture. *The English Journal, 91*(6), 88–92.
Morrison, T. (1970). *The bluest eye*. London, England: Vintage.
Murray, D. M. (1972). Teach writing as a process not product. *The Leaflet, 71*(3), 11–14.
Niche. (2015). The most diverse public high schools in New Jersey. Retrieved from https://k12.niche.com/rankings/public-high-schools/most-diverse/s/new-jersey/.
Perdomo, W. (1996). *Where a nickel costs a dime*. New York, NY: Norton.
Robinson, K. (2005). RSA animate—changing education paradigms. Retrieved from https://www.youtube.com/watch?v=zDZFcDGpL4U.
Rosal, P. (2015). The art of the mistake: Some notes on breaking as making. In *The breakbeat poets: New American poets in the age of hip-hop*. Chicago, IL: Haymarket Books. pp. 322–326.
Rose, T. (2008). *The hip hop wars: What we talk about when we talk about hip hop and why it matters*. New York, NY: Basic Civitas Books.
Sands, J. (2011). Yo (I need a beat). In *The new clean*. Long Beach, CA: Write Bloody.
Seidel, S. (2011). *Hip hop genius: Remixing high school education*. Lanham, MD: Rowman & Littlefield.
Shange, N. (1989). *For colored girls who have considered suicide when the rainbow is enuf: A choreopoem*. New York, NY: Collier Books.
Sweller, J. (1994). Cognitive load theory, learning difficulty, and instructional design. *Learning and Instruction, 4*, 295–312.
Walshe, R. D. (1979). What's basic to teaching writing? *English Journal, 68*(9), 51–56.
Williams, S. (2001). Coded language. On *Amethyst rock star* [CD]. Los Angeles, CA: American Recordings.

ABOUT THE AUTHOR

Brian Mooney is an educator, scholar, and author from New Jersey. He explores the intersections of Hip Hop, spoken word, literacy, and urban education. Brian holds a bachelor's degree from New York University and a master's degree from Teachers College, Columbia University, where he is currently pursuing his Ph.D. in English Education. His research considers the effects of Hip Hop culture on teaching and learning.

Brian is the founder and curator of *Word Up!*, a high school poetry slam that champions the voices of youth poets and MCs in Hudson County, NJ. The event has featured guest poets, rappers, and teaching artists including Kendrick Lamar, Patricia Smith, Andrea Gibson, Sarah Kay, and Rudy Francisco. Brian's work has been featured by national news outlets including *The New York Times*, *NBC*, *Rolling Stone*, *NPR*, *SiriusXM*, *MTV*, *Complex*, and others.

When he isn't grading papers, Brian enjoys making electronic music, writing poems, and spending time with his wife and their cat, Tigger, who is the coolest.

Studies in Criticality

General Editor
Shirley R. Steinberg

Counterpoints publishes the most compelling and imaginative books being written in education today. Grounded on the theoretical advances in criticalism, feminism, and postmodernism in the last two decades of the twentieth century, Counterpoints engages the meaning of these innovations in various forms of educational expression. Committed to the proposition that theoretical literature should be accessible to a variety of audiences, the series insists that its authors avoid esoteric and jargonistic languages that transform educational scholarship into an elite discourse for the initiated. Scholarly work matters only to the degree it affects consciousness and practice at multiple sites. Counterpoints' editorial policy is based on these principles and the ability of scholars to break new ground, to open new conversations, to go where educators have never gone before.

For additional information about this series or for the submission of manuscripts, please contact:

> Shirley R. Steinberg
> c/o Peter Lang Publishing, Inc.
> 29 Broadway, 18th floor
> New York, New York 10006

To order other books in this series, please contact our Customer Service Department:
> (800) 770-LANG (within the U.S.)
> (212) 647-7706 (outside the U.S.)
> (212) 647-7707 FAX

Or browse online by series:
> www.peterlang.com

www.ingramcontent.com/pod-product-compliance
Lightning Source LLC
Chambersburg PA
CBHW061350300426
44116CB00011B/2064